ome weeke...

Rushdie, comdemned to

...ey knew where to find him Friday ni... Knopf, wa...

... Grill, given by ~~Sonny~~ Sonny Mehta, pres. of Zebulo...

town. Rushdie, who turns out to be a pussycad, ...s

our most~~famous~~ famous writers, from Alice Adams to ~~...~~

~~...~~ You name 'em, they were there: Amy Tan,

e that up). Alice Walker, Ishmael Reed (th~~e~~se last two i

Lamott, Nobelist Czeslaw ~~Milzz~~ Milosz, ~~...~~

long feud), ~~Xxrixtrudy~~ Ethan Canin -- you g...

...ddy asked, "What would happen to our literary worl...

ed tonight?" A moment~~h~~'s ~~...~~ silence and then a successful nov...

e Steel would finally make number one on the local

stardah..

...~~Sure~~, a cheap shot but timing is everything. A...

...r put the knock on Willie Brown because he

...ch School whereas Mother Teres...

...sier to get fro...

in Ranch Mi... Yet an...
s Veretian Room... Yet an...
ony" (real name John Joseph Vidal Sr.) w...
e World Boxing Hall of Fame and a familiar figure ...
g was a major sport here. He wore a carnation daily...
pretty girl he saw.

STREET SCENE: stardush... Dennis Drayna caught the sightem a...
heavy traffic: the driver of a Smart Food Popcorn...
ddle lane, making a deal with the driver in the ti...
tting an armload of popcorn, the latter allowe...
his right turn... They do things differen...
took a ride on the freeway with...
82-
ay, and as she was about to change lan...
down there, and as she what you say down here -- (S...
ing "It's what you say down here... for look over your shoulder,
for look over shoulder,
the Sonora Uni...

The World of Herb Caen

THE WORLD OF
Herb Caen

SAN FRANCISCO
1938–1997

Edited by
Barnaby Conrad

Commentary and captions by
Carole Vernier

CHRONICLE BOOKS
SAN FRANCISCO

Special Thanks to Ann Moller Caen,
Jerry Bundsen, the San Francisco
Chronicle Library and Photo Department.

Introduction copyright ©1997
Barnaby Conrad

Copyright ©1997 by
The Chronicle Publishing Company

Printed in Hong Kong

Produced by Visual Strategies,
www.visdesign.com

Copy editing: Laura Merlo

Book design: Dennis Gallagher and
John Sullivan, Visual Strategies

Research: Paul Grady, Bruce Bellingham
and Jennifer Asche

Library of Congress Cataloging-in-
Publication Data available.

ISBN 0-8118-1859-4

Distributed in Canada by
Raincoast Books
8680 Cambie Street
Vancouver, B.C. V6P 6M9

10 9 8 7 6 5 4 3 2

Chronicle Books
85 Second Street
San Francisco, CA 94105

Web Site: www.chronbooks.com

The photographs in this volume are courtesy of the following sources. If there are any inaccuracies in the credits, the editors regret the oversights and will correct them in future printings. Please advise Chronicle Books of the correct information.

Photos courtesy of Barnaby Conrad, Ann Moller Caen, Maria Theresa Caen, Christopher Caen, Paul Grady, George Andros, and the San Francisco Chronicle.

Photographers:

Clem Albers: *38 and 39 spread, 102 left*

Peter Breinig: *8, 18, 36, 62 left, 95, 101 top*

Roland Calder: *109*

Bob Campbell: *27, 53, 88 and 89 spread, 92 left, 112 and 115 spread,*

Barnaby Conrad: *66 top*

Charles Denson: *88 right*

Art Downey: *12*

Susan Ehmer: *70 left*

Deanne Fitzmaurice: *10 bottom, 52 right, 72 left, 104 bottom*

Gary Fong: *75 left, 101 bottom*

Art Frisch: *30 and 31 spread, 32 left, 55*

Paul Grady: *10 bottom*

Jason Grow: *75 top*

Charles Hiller: *11 left*

Kem Lee Studio: *57*

Tom King: *37 right*

Fred Larson: *28 and 29 spread, 31 right, 78 and 79 spread, 106 and 107 spread*

Michael Macor: *90 right and 91 left spread*

Michael Maloney: *127 left*

John McBride: *126*

John O'Hara: *44 and 45 spread, 72 right, 77*

Gordon Peters: *100, 127 right*

Barney Peterson: *42 and 43 spread, 99, 115 right*

Steve Ringman: *124, 125 left*

Joe Rosenthal: *59, 98 bottom*

Terry Schmitt: *37 left, 105 right*

John Storey: *91 right, 102 and 103 spread*

Contents

Foreword

Herb Caen was a writer like no other, and I was blessed with the good taste to admire him without qualification. No one has ever covered the waterfront as well as this elegant, irascible man. His eye for detail was deadly, unmatchable and seemingly omniscient. It was a bad day to wake up an enemy of Herb Caen in San Francisco. But it was a glorious day to walk through the streets with your heels sparking off the pavement just right, when he had mentioned you kindly in that stream-of-consciousness prose, where Herb found both his voice and his art.

He taught the Americans who read him a different way to look at and measure a town. I know of no other writer whose name is also a synonym for the city he writes about. I think Herb gave the richest portrait of a city ever conceived by an American writer. His sense of place was as extraordinary as Balzac's, and his love of San Francisco rivaled the ardor that Tolstoy felt for Russia.

Herb Caen let me know how it felt to be alive during those sassy, high-spirited, fast-paced days when San Francisco was his town to do with as he liked. I think he was one of the great writers ever to come out of the American West. Few have written with as much pure brio as he has, or have given me as much sheer pleasure.

So I salute and praise and honor him. I lift a glass and think of the most beautiful city in the world, and how he helped define it, and shape it, and make love to it with a language that he swung like a blade. I write as a fan, a passionate fan of Herb Caen, and I offer him my heartfelt thanks, my thanks, my thanks.

Herb and his lifelong friend, author, artist and restaurateur Barnaby Conrad, bowl liquor bottles down with melons and coconuts outside Conrad's landmark bar, El Matador, in 1959.

Introduction

BY BARNABY CONRAD

In the old days, if Herb Caen's column wasn't in the morning newspaper, there was only one explanation:

It was Saturday.

For almost six decades starting on July 5, 1938 — and except for yearly vacations and a 3 $^{1}/_{2}$-year stint in the Army Air Force during World War II — Herb's column appeared, sparkling and infallible, to entertain and enlighten San Franciscans half a dozen times each and every week. In a typical year, he dropped 6,768 names, got 45,000 letters, 24,000 phone calls. If laid end to end, his columns would stretch 5.6 miles, from the Ferry Building to the Golden Gate Bridge. More than 16,000 columns of 1,000 words each! It is an astounding and unduplicated feat, by far the longest-running newspaper column in the country.

In the spring of 1996, several things happened. On April 3 Herb turned 80. Then in subsequent weeks he received the Pulitzer Prize, married his longtime sweetheart, Ann Moller, had a three-mile boulevard in his beloved city named after him, and June 14 was proclaimed Herb Caen Day. And that was some day, a uniquely San Franciscan happening. Seventy-five thousand people thronged in front of the Ferry Building to do him honor. All over the city martinis were marked down to the 25¢ price they commanded in 1916 when Herb was born. Squadrons of planes flew overhead, bands played, such celebrities as Walter Cronkite, Robin Williams, and Willie Mays spoke, famous singers sang, tap dancers tapped, and a joyous and profoundly moved Herb played the drums expertly with the Rich Martini Big Band. Said veteran newsman Cronkite to Herb as they rode in a fire engine from the fireboat station to Pier 23:

"If I hadn't seen it with my own eyes, I'd never have believed it — all these thousands of people turning out to cheer a newspaperman."

Over all the pomp and prizes and adulation hung Herb's chilling knowledge of his own mortality. He had told his readers at the end of May that he was undergoing chemotherapy and "hoped to pound out the column as long as possible."

> The point, dear friends and beloved enemies, is also like nothing I'd ever expected to experience. I have cancer.
>
> In a lightning flash I passed from the world of the well to the world of the unwell, where I hope to dwell for what I hope is a long time. The point is not to be maudlin or Pollyanna cheerful. This is serious stuff.

For a while he did three columns a week religiously, in or out of the pain and exhaustion of the treatments. Then one or two a week. Then more and more frequently a bleak little box appeared in the section of the paper where Herb had lived that stated: "Herb Caen will be writing from time to time."

In a late January telephone call to me, he said with a weak little laugh, "Hey, when's the remission supposed to kick in?"

The day before he died, the editor of The San Francisco Chronicle, Bill German, went to see him in the hospital. Herb was unable to speak, but he made typing motions with his fingers and smiled as though promising him one more column, a promise his failing body wouldn't let him keep.

He died early the next morning, February first. The city's flags flew at half mast. His funeral was held at a jammed Grace Cathedral, followed that evening by a candlelight march from South Beach to Aquatic Park on Herb Caen Way. San Francisco was in mourning. Even Macy's, which for years had run the full-length ad next to his column, ran a heartfelt paean to Herb's absence.

Over the years, Herb had little competition in San Francisco and only one true rival. That came in 1949 from a columnist named Robert Patterson who wrote flamboyantly and well for The San Francisco Examiner. "They hired him out of jail," Herb remembered. "They misunderstood his letter. They thought he was with Time in Atlanta. Well, he was *doing* time in Atlanta.

"He was very hard to write a column against because he'd print anything. I said, 'Bob, you're really killing me.' And he said, 'Yeah, but I'm killing myself, day by day, because I'm not going to have any sources left by the time I'm through. Give me three years, kid, and the town's yours again.' And, true enough, he didn't last three years."

Over the next decades there were several other challengers, but Herb was unique and remained unrivaled.

I've been honored when Herb has referred to me in his column as his "oldest and best friend," but we do not go back

Doing his KPO radio column
in the late 1930s, left.
Picking out his uniform to go
off to war in 1942, above.

'Isn't it nice that people who prefer Los Angeles to San Francisco live there?'

to childhood; I was a feisty 18 when I met the already famous Herb Caen at a debutante party in Hillsborough in 1940, a sad little affair since there was only one deb that year because of the impending war. My name first made the column in 1941 when I stowed away on a Matson liner bound for Hawaii with my beauteous cousin, was discovered in Los Angeles, and kicked off the ship. Herb and I continued our friendship at Yale, where I was an undergraduate and where Herb was in officers training school for the Air Corps. After the war, I found myself back in San Francisco trying to be a writer, always with Herb's interest and support. No matter how inept a book or article I wrote, Herb would give it a mention, even if his uncompromising standards would only allow him a plug of the "Well, that *is* a baby" variety.

After my book "Matador" became a runaway best-seller in 1952, I decided to open an elegant bar-nightclub in the North Beach section of San Francisco. Herb was the first in the door and was such a regular customer that we gave him his own table with a small brass plaque on it. Single-handedly, he made my saloon the place to go by recording the doings and sayings of the many celebrities who frequented the spot. Herb himself brought in such stars as William Saroyan, André Previn, Frank Sinatra, Truman Capote, and John Huston. Worldly, sophisticated, well-read, and gregarious, he seemed to know everyone in the world; he somehow made them honorary San Franciscans, and let us, his readers, have the privilege of knowing them, too.

Life in those days, officially known as the Good Old Days, seemed to center around the Prado, the hungry i, Vanessi's, New Joe's, the Buena Vista, Jack's, Al Williams' Papagayo Room, Trader Vic's, and the Lower Mark bar. Enrico's was the place for action at lunch over endless rounds of "The Match Game," and what wonderful items came out of

Enrico and Sue Banducci dine with Herb and art dealer Billy Pearson in the 1960s, above.

Glenn Dorenbush, John Cordoni and Carole Vernier at Jimmy Lyons' memorial jazz tribute at Bimbo's in April 1994, below.

there. I happened to witness a scene that became a classic Caen item. John Steinbeck came to San Francisco on the final lap of driving his camper around the United States, the basis of his best-selling book "Travels With Charley." We were at Enrico's sidewalk café, and Charley, the big black poodle, sat obediently in a corner near our table. With us were Herb and Howard Gossage, the innovative advertising man. Oh, to have had a tape recorder and been able to catch the sound as well as the words of the following dialogue! John growled out his sentences in unique ursine grunts while Howard's congenital stammer heightened rather than hampered his wit.

"Look at that dog over there," said John morosely. "Yesterday in the great redwoods of Muir Woods he lifted his leg on a tree that was twenty feet across, a hundred feet high, and a thousand years old. Howard, Howard! What's left in life for that poor dog?"

Howard thought of the terrible dilemma for a moment and then said, "Well, J-J-John, he could always t-t-teach!"

Herb always seemed to be at the right place to catch the bon mot at the right time. In Normandy, for example, a few hours after the horrendous D-Day landings, he had to go to the bathroom. Approaching a quintessential old Frenchman in a smock and beret, he asked, *"Monsieur, s'il vous plait, où est le lavabo?"* The old man flung open his grateful arms and with tears in his eyes exclaimed, *"Mais, toute la belle France, mon ami, toute la belle France!"*

Not just San Francisco but all the world has been fodder for Herb's columns, from Paris to Cairo and London to China. No travel writer I know could make you feel a foreign place so quickly and in such telling detail. In 1959, Herb came to visit my wife and me in Tahiti, discovered snorkeling and a lovely island girl with the improbable name of Nita Wanamaker, and wrote six memorable articles about that then-relatively unknown island. In Spain, Herb and I went to the corrida in Malaga with Orson Welles — and the bull jumped the barrier and landed in Orson's copious lap. "The animal quickly realized its predicament and got back into the arena," reported Herb.

On a jaunt to Tijuana, we saw Arruza put up a great display of skill and courage for an enthralled crowd. One woman got so carried away that as the handsome matador circled the arena in triumph, she stood up and threw her bra down to him — an act that Herb described as "an empty gesture if I ever saw one!" On our return airplane flight, Herb became curious about the little porcelain "Atomic Pig" he'd bought from a sidewalk vendor: All on its own, its ears wiggled and its tail wagged. Herb broke it open to learn the mystery, and five angry bees stormed out, to the near-panic of the stewardesses and passengers. Another great column was born for us to enjoy over breakfast: "Bees in the Afternoon."

While Herb was known for his "Chronicling" of the immediate, he was unequaled as a writer of obituaries. His ability to capture the essence of a person's life in a few paragraphs was demonstrated superbly in a column dedicated to the complicated actor Sterling Hayden, as well as in his eulogies to Trader Vic, Mayor George Moscone, Benny Goodman, William Saroyan, and dozens of others. He cared about these people and made his readers care, too.

One of Herb's great joys was finding anecdotes about old San Francisco that were both historical and funny, such as:

Robert Louis Stevenson was lunching with a friend at the Poodle Dog, and telling him that San Francisco waiters never admit they don't have everything that's on the menu. "Why," smiled Stevenson, "they'll take your order for a slice of the moon, come back and tell you they're just out of it. Look, I'll show you."

Turning to the waiter, he ordered, "A double order of broiled behemoth, please."

"Rare or well done?" dead-panned the waiter.

"Well done," said R.L.S. with a wink at his friend. A few minutes later the waiter returned to announce, "We are out of the behemoth." Then he leaned over confidentially. "To tell the truth," he whispered, "we do have some, but I wouldn't want to serve it to you, Mr. Stevenson. It isn't fresh."

And, of course, anecdotes about the families of Old San Francisco were sheer joy, as with this bit of serendipity: Once, the brash young Caen tried to introduce an heiress from the de Young family, which owned The Chronicle, to an heiress from the Spreckels family, which owned sugar mills and much else. "Oh, we know each other," said the de Young heiress. "It's just that we haven't spoken since her daddy shot my daddy."

One of Herb's other pleasures in writing the column was seeing what he could sneak by his editors — his "naughties." He was inordinately proud of this one about a San Franciscan who went into FAO Schwarz at Christmastime looking for a Barbie doll for his daughter:

"Does Barbie come with Ken?" he asked the perky saleswoman.

"Actually no," she answered slyly, "Barbie comes with G.I. Joe — she fakes it with Ken."

And:

Contrary to the North Beach rumors, it's not true that Coit Tower is in love with the Broadway Tunnel!

And the famous, now politically incorrect, one that titillated readers so many years ago, about the owner of the

Barnaby Conrad, Eve Arden and Herb judge a fortune cookie contest at Trader Vic's in 1958, above. Owner Victor Bergeron canceled the contest, deeming the entries too risque. Herb with second wife, Sally Gilbert, at an opera opening in the 1950s, left.

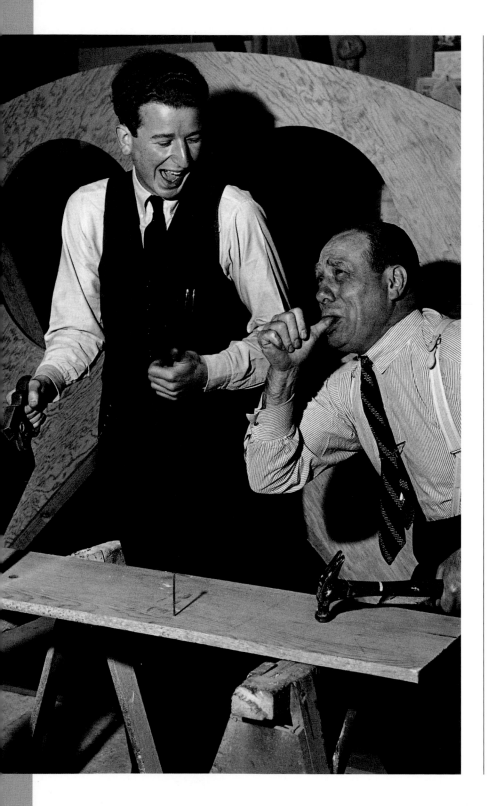

celebrated drag queen nightclub on Broadway: "Joe Finocchio must be the only man who lives off the labor of his fruits."

In his columns Herb seldom told jokes of the standard variety. Often they were just anecdotes, homey, everyday happenings of the type that get reprinted in The Reader's Digest, such as this:

> Fed up with too many homework assignments, a 10-year-old aspiring actress at Marin Country Day School near San Francisco complained to her Spanish teacher, but to no avail. Finally the girl looked her teacher in the eye and stated darkly, "You will not be thanked when I receive my Academy Award."

Longtime readers came to expect many Herbisms, such as his Namephreaks, viz:

> And then there are the namephreaks, worse luck. Step up to meet Pam Talkington, spokeswoman for the Memorial Hospital in Modesto (Dan Campbell). Bob Sparks wonders if you've heard about the Sacramento periodontist named Dr. Ronald R. Rott. Mr. Fillin is a substitute teacher at Woodside Elementary. Ann Ellingson phoned Cheese Please in B'linggame and was charmed to hear, "Cheese Please, Brie speaking." 'Twas Brie Mercis, who is already tired of the runny drippy jokes. Prof. Ralph E. Kunkee of UC Davis notes that the Vatican spokesman for its latest decree against rock 'n' roll is one Cardinal Rapsong and that is why namephreaks will always be with us. Cheers!

He often said he hated Namephreaking and swore he would not ever run another one, and then a few weeks later something like this would appear:

> Era's end: At last! Shirley Nice, who conducted a seminar titled, 'How to Handle People with Tact and Skill,' has retired after at least 25 years. She was one of the first

namephreaks and certainly the one most submitted. She now enters the Namephreak Hall of Fame, along with S.F. piano teacher Patience Scales; Firmin Gryp, the glad-handing bank president; Philander Beadle, the divorce lawyer; and ol' Doc Kneebone, specialist in that very joint.

And then his celebrated, perennial, choleric tirade against turkeys, the feathered kind, which crusade always came to a boil, quite naturally, at Thanksgiving time.

He always decried his annual Christmas poem but continued to write it to celebrate the names of his friends from all walks of life, the many loyal people who throughout the year supply him with "ites" — as he called the items, news, and anecdotes that they sent or called in. His 1997 column that appeared on his last Christmas day, starts out:

> One More Time
> Oh, I lied but I really tried
> To kill this annual crashing bore:
> Thuh Christmas poem with names galore ...

It goes on in a more somber vein — remember he had learned only eight months earlier that he had inoperable cancer.

> I started this pome in '41;
> The world was young, the city fun
> And run by people of incredible grandeur
> Who took pity on the Sackamenna Kid
> And said sure, they'd love to see their names
> In Thuh Christmas Pome and associated games
> And thus a tradition was born:
> Fifty-five years of unabashed corn.
> Last year I killed it lightly,
> Saying the old dog had run its course,
> But this year I feel differently about

Herb and third wife, Maria Theresa, keep their cool as other fans lose their grip at the 1965 Beatles concert at the Cow Palace, above.

With Armand Girard, KGO–KPO singer, preparing for the station's puppet show at a fair in the late 1930s, previous page.

Herb touts parasols as one solution to the 'pigeon fallout' problem in Union Square in October 1962. The event was the brainstorm of Herb's longtime friend, publicist Tony Kent.

Life and death and tradition:
Let us cling to one another as long as we can
In a world grown old and cold.

He ended the doggerel with some jaunty gallows humor:

Uh-oh, here come the guys with the stretcher:
"Merry Christmas, everybody, nice to have metcher!"

He loved to play with words, and many of his coinages were memorable, such as referring to the Bay Bridge as "the car-strangled spanner." Some stuck, such as renaming the aggressive lawyer Melvin Belli "Mr. Bellicose," City Hall as "Silly Hall," and Willie Brown as "Da Mayor." And of course, "Sackamenna," "Berserkeley," and "Baghdad-by-the-Bay."

But it was the term "beatnik" to define members of the Beat Generation that instantly became part of everyone's vocabulary around the world. Notice how casually Herb tosses it off, as though the word had been around for years:

Look magazine, preparing a picture spread on S.F.'s Beat Generation (oh, no, not AGAIN!), hosted a party in a No. Beach house for 50 Beatniks, and by the time word got around the sour grapevine, over 250 bearded cats and kits were on hand, slopping up Mike Cowles' free booze. They're only Beat, y'know, when it comes to work.

Every San Franciscan has some favorite items from the column. I like the quote from the aging lothario and film director Jean Negulesco, who said: "Oh yes, I still chase girls, but I am so grateful when they say no."

And the line from writer Frances Weaver: "Every morning when I wake up I decide whether today I'm going to be the statue or the pigeon."

And one of my all-time favorites, which I'll have to do from memory — after all, there are 16,000-plus columns, and I can't find it. It's about humorist James Thurber, when his doctor told him that he had "sugar in his urine and a murmur in his heart." Retorted Thurber: "That's not a diagnosis, that's a song cue!"

And still another:

When told by a friend that he was planning a trip to the Philippines, Paul Lazarus, a professor at the University of California at Santa Barbara, suggested flying Garuda, Indonesia's national airline. His friend shook his head, saying: "I make it a policy never to fly on airlines where the pilots believe in reincarnation."

And another one from memory:

Now we're in Paris at that city's finest fishing tackle shop. In comes Jack Hemingway, world-class trout fisherman, Ernest's oldest son. After buying several items from the elegant salesman, Jack gave him his credit card. "Ah, Hemingway," he said. "Me, I am Tolstoy!" And indeed he was — Count Leo's grandson.

Besides his newsy items, Herb was well known for his poetic elegies of the city he loved, such as this fragment from May 5, 1953:

An extravagant sunset fading so fast that you can't fully enjoy all the work that must have gone into it, a lone white sail fluttering home at dusk past the amber lights of the bridge that only a dreamer could have built, the ceaseless nighttime hum of life and tires and lights and horns in this worldly town that never quite finds time to go to sleep, and then — the moon rising fast out of the far-off East to beam whitely down on the hills and valleys and restless waters of the tiny city that has no boundaries. . . . San Francisco. Ah, San Francisco.

Herb Caen's funeral, at 10:30 on Friday, February 7, 1997, was unique in the city's history, indeed perhaps in the history of any city. It was estimated that 2,500 people jammed the majestic Grace Cathedral on Nob Hill, and hundreds more gathered outside to hear the eulogies and music over loudspeakers.

There was Brahms played on the piano by the conductor of the San Francisco Symphony Orchestra; there was a great clarinetist playing Herb's favorite song, "What's New," a fine young opera star gave us an aria from "Tosca," the clarinetist played Benny Goodman's melancholy theme song, "Good-bye," and the service ended with the joyous Dixieland band of Turk Murphy.

As we were leaving the cathedral, Enrico Banducci, who had come from Virginia for the services, said huskily: "This is the damnedest saddest, most wonderful funeral anyone ever had, but the only man who could properly describe it isn't here."

Interspersed with the music, several distinguished people spoke, among them Mayor Willie Brown; Herb's longtime editor, Bill German; and actor Robin Williams. They each said a heartfelt goodbye to their friend in a different manner. And for the next days and weeks letters poured in to The Chronicle, and many touching ones were printed. Professor Shelly

At the Fairmont Hotel with his beloved Ann
Moller at the black-tie dinner party honoring
his 75th birthday in April 1991.

Lowenkopf said: "Herb did for San Francisco what Samuel Pepys did for London, what Boswell did for Johnson, and what Sears did for Roebuck. . . ."

A young novelist said, "It's true, as Hartley maintained, that the past is a foreign country — and it's equally true that Herb Caen had the number one gilt-edged passport to San Francisco's past. . . ."

For me, one of the letters that most hit home was from one Frank Berkenkotter from Guinda, Yolo County:

> Editor — I want to report a "Herb sighting." We were walking north on Jones, coming back from ACT, and there he was, Herb, a block away, walking down Vallejo. When we got to the top of Vallejo and Jones, the fog obscured our view, and he was gone.
>
> On drippy nights, when the foghorn blows, I can feel Herb rolling in at 2 a.m., walking the top of Russian Hill. Herb is here. The shadow knows.

Someone once said that San Francisco was "a city that invented itself." Maybe so. But it had an awful lot of help from a writer named Herbert Eugene Caen.

"He has made a many-faceted character of the city of San Francisco," said John Steinbeck, years ago. "It is very probable that Herb's city will be the one that is remembered."

What follows are anecdotes — "items" Herb called the gems that daily poured from his "tripewriter" — which have been selected because they capture the pulse of his beloved city, or for no other reason then that they caught the fancy of the editor.

Herb's own caption for this photo: 'Yes, that is indeed the legendary Don Sherwood in the center, smiling through tears. The scene is Bay Meadows and I had just beaten him in a one-on-one sulky race. A sulky is a pair of wheels with a small seat that gives you a wonderful view of a real horse's ass. The horses, which are trotters, occasionally look back and make the same remark. The wonderful fellow on the right is Joe Cohen, an owner of the track. Shall we say 1961?'

TV series, "Bl... --a black woman wearing a D... three chess players, saying "The one who b... Why a mayoress? Because this scene w... missioner"... "Da mayor" is played by L.A. actress Candy Br... ago. "Da mayor" is played by L.A. actress Candy Br... a stretch from Willie Brown Mineola... Willie was... ut said "I don't do drag." by... said "I don't do drag." stardash...

The Walking Caen

Speaking of which! Jack and Jennie Castor of San F... ue Train from Johannesburg to Capetown, were hande... tions, printed in English and Afrikaans, and when they c... laughed, "Are we still in California?" (Yeah, "Dra... s")... And getting back to the Geary Theater, take... w glories you can get these days for a mere $2... that glories of the word. However, the opening... ree of the word... should've been honor... of FEMA...

Full Moon Rising

And a full moon rising over the
Bay remains one of the world's
most breathtaking sights.
On a recent night from
Telegraph Hill, it looked like a
great orange balloon, tied to the
Bridge by an invisible string.
It hovered there forever, then
suddenly broke away and rose
swiftly. In its eventual whiteness,
it belonged to everybody, but for
a few harsh eternal moments,
it was our very own.

NOVEMBER 1965

The Ferry Building at midnight,
November 8, 1973, with a few
cars streaking over the
Embarcadero Freeway and the
Bay Bridge and the bay
shimmering in the background.

Previous page: This 1960s photo of Herb on
Telegraph Hill was taken by his then
brother-in-law, Mason Weymouth, who was
married to Herb's older sister Estelle.

Limos and Cable Cars

MAY 19, 1994

These are the nights of long limos. The blacked-out stretchers, longer than hearses and twice as lively, are rolling between the hotels, the restaurants and the clubs, disgorging their high school graduates, the girls already looking grown up and in charge, the boys acting silly. Let 'em. These are the best times of their endless days and long nights, filled with laughter and new memories to be stored for future reference: "Omigod, were we ever really that young?" The date for these gloriously coltish young people is The First of Everything: first love, first white tux jacket (can't stop staring in the mirror), first white lie, first double-cross, maybe even first martini. Middle age begins soon enough — the first kid, the first mortgage, maybe even the last martini — and then for the rest of their young lives, more middle age, for in California, nobody gets old, only older.

Limos and cable cars in the city of outstretched palms and the changeless chants of "Spare change?" I'm a pushover, but when I get a $25 parking ticket because I was out of quarters for the meter, I wonder if the change was so spare after all. The tourists here and the lines are long again at the Market-Powell turntable. Welcome to the land of the summer fog, dear new friends in your neat washables. We who live here worry that the city might not measure up to the myths we blithely disseminate, but I guess we're our own severest critics. On the topmost corners of Nob Hill, I see tourists go crazy. Standing in the intersections, they whirl like dervishes as they shoot photos in four directions: hills, valleys, distant peaks, the cables, the bay, Alcatraz and Angel, sailboats and freighters, Chinatown's pagoda'd roofs, a snatch of the Bay Bridge. From their antics, you can tell they've never seen anything like this before and they are entranced. The jaded San Franciscan looks twice and becomes entranced all over again.

Pondering these imponderables, I walk along 11th St. It is twilight, my favorite time, dry with a hint of vermouth. I am in love with the city all over again. Over on 10th and Howard, the golden salt-and-pepper shaker towers of St. Joseph's shine in the dying sun. The church is doomed as well as domed, a victim of one of the most hateful split infinitives: "to better serve you!" It's one we hear all the time. Banks close your favorite branch and "consolidate" with one 20 blocks away "to better serve you." Stores that were once open seven days a week now close on weekends "to better serve you." Archbishop Quinn, certainly a fine man, is closing or "consolidating" parishes (i.e., closing churches) "to better serve you" and you better believe it. You are being serviced. Hallelujah, Alleluia, let the mighty organ rise...

Walking east on 11th, warmed by a merely passable martinus (singular) in a Mission deadfall that opens at 6 a.m. each day for those to whom breakfast is a boilermaker. It's a San Francisco tradition, going back to the age of blue-collar workers,

. . .
25

red of face, strong of union and breath. If I walked east long enough, would I get to Oakland or San Leandro? Drown, most likely, but I was feeling reasonably immortal. Don't think I've ever been in San Leandro. Closest I got was when I was seated in the right field bleachers at the Oakland Coliseum during the '89 World Series. That was when the A's were the A's, not the ZZZzzz's. Still it's hard not to admire Tony La Russa. To rephrase W.C. Fields, a man who likes ballet and homeless animals can't be all bad but how does he really feel about guys who get $5 million a year and don't hit their own weight?

Why was I on 11th Street? (*Get off it — Ed.*) My ancient car, the infamous White Rat, was in the hospital again at Bay European, its transmission in even worse shape than my own. As I walked along, contemplating the worst of all possible sellouts (a Lexus), a pigeon fell into step with me. No, but seriously. We walked along in silence, which is a good thing. A geezer gabbing with a pigeon could confirm a lot of rumors, best expressed by placing your index finger at your forehead and revolving it rapidly. Two old city birds, one with red feet from walking all day on the hard pavement. The pigeon's feet didn't look so good, either. (You saw that coming.) I toyed with the idea of putting a leash on the bird and walking it around town, in the manner of the Parisian poet Gerard de Nervil, who had a pet lobster on a leash. "It doesn't eat much," he explained, "and it knows the secrets of the deep." I stamped my foot and the pigeon flew off. Back to its nest. Pigeons mate for life and the males lactate. How's that for a secret?

Back on Powell, once the heartbeat of a stylish city, now funky. "When asked which words in the English language are the most difficult to define precisely, a lexicographer would surely mention 'funky.'" So reads a note in the American Heritage Dictionary, and yet we use the word all the time, blindly or deafly. "Soulful, down to earth," ventures the lexicographer, adding "grungy clothes. Perhaps the Latin 'fumigare.' See 'fumigate.'" Hey, what are you trying to tell us here? I continued up the street, in a funk about funkiness. There is no longer any Frisco Jazz on the streets of San Francisco. A harmonica player was growling something sad. I turned into the Gold Dust, my favorite funky place for a nightcap and a pickup (no, not that kind). A banjo, a trombone, a trumpet, a piano and a lot of good vibes. Barbara the waitress said, "The usual?" and I nodded. There are no secrets in this old town.

Paper, Please

Why I say Matrix isn't working: This, the 14th largest city in the country, has the fourth largest number of so-called homeless, and the gantlet of paper-cupped pitifuls gets longer and longer. I'm still good for a quarter but that pittance doesn't go as far as it used to. "Paper money, please."

OCTOBER 9, 1995

Glory Days

Barbary Coast dives were gaudy and bawdy, run by some of the most hard-boiled yeggs ever to poach their way through the dirty politics of the day.

NOVEMBER 29, 1987

The area bounded by Kearny, Columbus, Washington, Sansome and Pacific was known as the Barbary Coast, the wickedest part of San Francisco. It boasted 24 saloons and dance halls in the 500 block of Pacific alone. After the 1906 earthquake and fire burned it to the ground, the Barbary Coast became the somewhat more respectable International Settlement, still an area of nightclubs and saloons but with an artistic and bohemian community. Then Prohibition wiped out the drinking establishments.

Weather Report

Gray Line buses hauling gray-faced tourists through the gray city on a gray day, a city crew washing the Broadway Tunnel as the rain splashes outside, Chinese selling Japanese trinkets to South Americans carrying German cameras ... gee, what a crazy town.

JANUARY 31, 1960

* * *

Ahh, S.F. "When we start getting perfect football weather," observes Henry Berman, "you can tell that baseball season is about to begin."

MARCH 30, 1960

St. Ignatius Church in the Richmond District poking through the fog opposite Lone Mountain College at right.

Heavenly Daze

Loud cries of "Snow! Snow!" at 6 a.m. yesterday on our usually quiet street. Kids tumbling out in parkas for snowball fights, their elders flashing cameras. Immediate bicentennial colors: red noses, white breath, blue ears. A neighbor's French poodle, let out for its morning constitutional, hit the icy stairs and skidded hilariously to the sidewalk, legs flying; as we laughed, it looked offended and French. The cherry blossoms that had emerged prematurely tucked pink heads back under limbs. Putting on overcoat, muffler, gloves, and pasting a "Ski Transamerica Pyramid!" sticker on my bumper, I headed South on Webster, glorying in the white silence of distant San Bruno Mt.

FEBRUARY 6, 1976

The Golden Gate Bridge leads the way to the Marin Headlands on the morning of February 5, 1976.

The Famous Shortcut

Some Kind of Weekend: It was raining pitchforks, cats and dogs and/or violets Friday (pick one), and there I was at Le Central with no Burberry or bumbershoot. Shortcut time! Take deep breath and — dash up Bush through Sutter-Stockton Garage, fight traffic to Hyatt Union Square, cross into Union Square Garage, fly over Geary, skid into Macy's, scamper down escalator, exit on O'Farrell into O'Farrell-Ellis garage, take elevator down to Ellis, whoosh into Woolworth's (terrible chicken smell), leap headlong down steps into basement, run through Powell-Market BART station to Emporium's new basement (Market on Market, terrific), go up rear escalator to rear exit, cross Jessie into Giannini's Market, scuttle through (holding nose) and arrive at Chronicle reasonably dry. Yes, this entails a lot of jaywalking. And if The Chronicle isn't where you wanted to go why didn't you say so?

NOVEMBER 17, 1981

**The Transamerica building
is reflected in the rain.**

. . .

31

Herb railed against many architectural eyesores in San Francisco – the Bank of America monolith, the Transamerica Pyramid (below), huge hotels like the Marriott and Ramada Renaissance, to name a few – and was particularly enraged by what he called the Dambarcadero, the Embarcadero Freeway overpass that cut off the view of the bay along the Waterfront. When it was damaged in the 1989 earthquake, Herb wasted no time in suggesting it be demolished. In 1990 he wrote: "Say, what are we waiting for, anyway? Let's start tearing down the Dambarcadero Freeway now and open up the surface roadway. Forget such complexities as tunnels. Keep it simple, stupid." The overpass was indeed torn down, though it took several years. And on June 14, 1996, the sweeping sidewalk next to the Embarcadero roadway was named 'Herb Caen Way.'

Herb truly loathed the Vaillancourt Fountain (above) in Justin Hermann Plaza, calling it '10 on the Richter Scale' and begging that it be torn down when the Embarcadero Freeway was demolished. It wasn't.

He also appreciated architecture critic Allan Temko's assessment of the piece as looking like 'a deposit made by a dog with square intestines.'

Telegraph Hill with the Embarcadero freeway in the background, 1961.

In One Ear

Overheard at the Circus Lounge: "Let's go over to the Mark and be indifferent."

AUGUST 4, 1938

Unbridled Ambition

One of my pet ambitions is to run screaming through the lobby of the Fairmont, bowling old ladies off their red plush perches and tweaking the noses of aged elevator boys.

FEBRUARY 20, 1940

Steam Heat

Interested tourist to Powell cable grip man: "And what heating system do you use on these cars?" Grip man: "Togetherness."

JANUARY 6, 1960

Steep Grade

Speaking of such, Melissa Feldberg nominates for oblivion the many signs around our town that proclaim "HILL" on what is quite clearly a hill. I particularly liked the one at the top of Filbert St. precipice that bore a graffitic "No ****!"

APRIL 5, 1996

Herb waits for a cable car at the corner of California and Powell streets, circa 1954.

Age of Aquarius

At B'way and Columbus,
Herb the Furrier
overheard one beat ask
another: "Hey, you gotta
TV set?" "Not me, man,"
came the reply.
"I take LSD and watch
the wallpaper."

DECEMBER 21, 1965

**A beatnik reads among
what The Chronicle of
March 18, 1964, referred
to as 'the paraphernalia
of Bohemianism.'**

Dancers in Washington Square with Sts. Peter and Paul Church in background, 1975.

Square Heart

As Kevin Wallace once wrote, Washington Square, which isn't square, is the heart of North Beach, which isn't a beach, and has a statue of Benjamin Franklin, not Washington.

OCTOBER 13, 1992

Herb has Sunday brunch at a table in front of Enrico's with model Sue Barton in 1959.

Each year on April 18 survivors of the 1906 earthquake, along with a stalwart band of early risers and numerous firemen, arrive before 5 a.m. at Lotta's Fountain at Battery and Market streets, as in this 1976 photo. Speeches are made, survivors recount earthquake legends. At 5:13, the moment of the first 1906 temblor, a band strikes up 'San Francisco' and everyone weeps, cheers and drinks to the occasion. Herb loved the event and always wrote it up, commenting sadly each year on the dwindling number of survivors. One year he complimented the firemen on the quality of the Bloody Marys they served that morning, causing an overly sensitive chief to cut them off the following year. Dark muttering about lynching Herb was heard, but the following year Bloody Marys were discreetly being poured again.

Lotta's Fountain

"The Survivors," a brave and dwindling band, will show up yet again at Lotta's Fountain, to stand in silence at 5:13 a.m., the moment of the 1906 earthquake that still casts a strange spell over the city. It's a sincere event in an age of phony "happenings." No commercialization, no slickness, no "party planning." It's folksy, in the way I imagine San Francisco was in 1906, despite the grandeur of the old Palace Hotel across the street. Nobody puttin' on the ritz or the dog. Just a lot of ordinary extraordinary people who are revered to this day. They watched their beloved city burn down and couldn't wait to build another that would be even better. They're heroes because we're not quite sure, even after October 1989, that we could measure up. The condition of our freeways, almost three years later, tends to confirm that doubt.

APRIL 16, 1992

Hell on Wheels

People hate bike messengers. I love 'em.
They're dangerous and they live
dangerously, all in the service of capitalism,
consumerism or whatever you want to call
it. OK, business. These kids are possibly
radicals, and here they are risking life and
limb — theirs and ours — to get those
papers, packages and messages from one
office to another, as fast and unsafely as
possible. Devotion to duty, by golly.
They've got it. That, and something that is
fast disappearing from our drab little
corporate world of paper-pushers and
bean-counters. They are colorful.

JULY 30, 1989

Missing Persons

No mystery about the 60,288
San Franciscans missing in the census.
They're all down in Union Square Garage
waiting for their cars.

JUNE 16, 1960

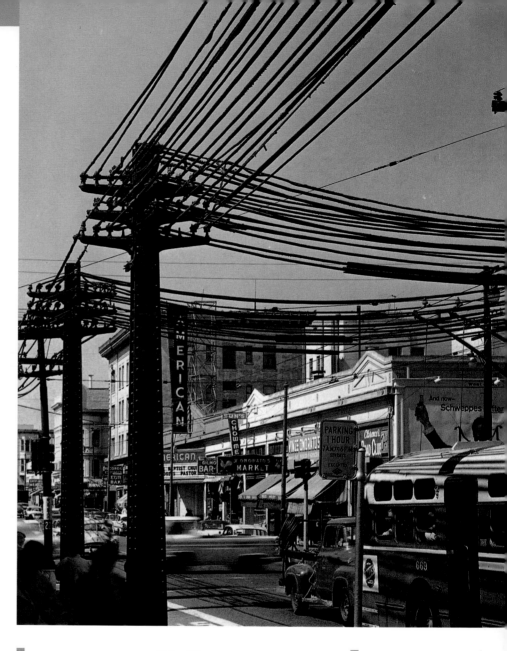

Skin-Tight

Joe Piccinini squeezed his car between two
others in a Safeway lot, inched his way out, and
came back to find a note on his windshield.
"I hope one of these days *you* get pregnant and
someone parks that close to you!"

On August 4, 1977, 40 Asian tenants were evicted from the International Hotel at Columbus and Jackson, a subsidized housing project that the city wanted to tear down. Herb called it 'the infamous symbol of the city's heartlessness,' but the issue lost at the polls in November and the hotel was razed in 1979.

Traffic congestion on the corner of Fillmore and Turk Streets, 1964.

The Sophisticated Traveler

Old San Francisco, repository of freedom, tolerance and understanding. The International Hotel at Kearny and Jackson, whose fate is in the voters' hands tomorrow as low-cost housing for elderly Filipinos and Chinese, was once "The Best Hotel in San Francisco!" That's what it says in a full-page ad found by litterateur Lew Ferbrache in F.W. Warner's "Guide to San Francisco," published in 1882. . . . We read of the rates ($1 to $1.50 per night), the laundry facilities (Hot and Cold Baths), and finally, the ultimate inducement to the sophisticated traveler: "No Chinese Employed In Or About the Hotel."

NOVEMBER 7, 1977

. . .

41

Photo Opportunity, Poignant:

The three homeless men who sleep nightly in the doorway at 222 Front. Each morning, notes passerby Donna Chaban, two are still asleep while the third is propped up in his sleeping bag, watching "Good Morning, America!" on a tiny TV.

AUGUST 12, 1988

Life Is A Cabaret

Last Fri., Howard Young passed a beggar on the sidewalk at Mish' and New Montgy., a violin and a sleeping dog beside him. After giving him a buck, Howard pointed to the fiddle and asked, "How about a tune?" "No," replied the mendicant. "I don't wanna wake up my dog."

NOVEMBER 2, 1981

This warehouse at 734 Howard Street was among the many buildings demolished in December 1981 to make room for the controversial Yerba Buena project. Part of Yerba Buena Gardens now stands on this spot.

· 42 ·

Onward to New Lows

Will it make any difference who's elected mayor today? I've been thinking back over the mayors I've known, from "Sunny Jim" to Rossi, Lapham, Elmer Robinson, Shelley, the lovable Moscone and so on, and I'd have to say not much. Maybe George Christopher, Alioto and Dianne made a difference, being strong, but when you reflect on the Embarcadero Freeway, Candlestick Park and Manhattanization, you have to wonder.

DECEMBER 10, 1991

Long Gone

The day Frankie Flier drove his Cadillac into the parking lot at Seventh and Mission and with his lawyer started to cross the street to Federal Court, "How long will you be gone?" the attendant called after him. "About five years," answered Frankie, who a few minutes later pleaded guilty to a narcotics charge and was sentenced to —
10 years.

FEBRUARY 28, 1960

Two South of Market denizens, which Herb called 'Skid Rowgues,' enjoy a libation at the corner of Sixth and Natoma streets in 1974; under graffiti dedicated to Herb Caen. The area was (and still is to some extent) a conglomeration of cheap hotels and decaying warehouses.

Don't Call It Frisco

The first time Ogden Nash came to S.F., circa 1940, a Chronicle
reporter challenged him to produce a clever couplet on San Francisco
and it didn't take him longer than 30 seconds to recite "May I be boiled
in oil and fried in Crisco/If I ever call San Francisco Frisco,"
but I think he had it up his sleeve.

MARCH 14, 1995

. . .

A Salty Nickname

Somebody from the Marin Independent Journal phoned me a few days ago to ask how I felt about the growing use of "Frisco," I having written a book called "Don't Call It Frisco," and I said it don't make me no never mind any longer. I don't care what people call us as long as they call us, besides which "Frisco" is a salty nickname, redolent of the days when we had a bustling waterfront.

APRIL 22, 1993

· · ·

Herb's war with Chico began in 1973 when he innocently published an item from a reader who said that Chico was the kind of town where you found Velveeta in the gourmet section of the supermarket. This developed into a long-running joke between Chico and Herb. Few "Cheekoites" took it seriously; in fact, Chico State College made hay on it for years, eventually daring Herb to come up for the dedication of their campus theater, an event he attended with alacrity. His frequent promise to swear off the Velveeta jokes was broken more times than anyone can remember. In a way, everything outside San Francisco, unable to live up to its glorious neighbor, could be considered Velveetaland.

Lee Nye, program director of KK105 in Sacramento, is about to make a fortune in Chico with his new product: Velveeta on a rope for those who get hungry in the shower. . . Ken McEldowney is ecstatic that Velveeta now comes in extra thick slices. "Now," he goes on, "if only someone would market white bread with the crust already trimmed"

＊ ＊ ＊

Len Sullivan of P'Alto checked into the Royal Windsor in Brussels and ordered the continental breakfast, which arrived with only one cheese. Yup. Chico, yr magical smell is everywhere!

JUNE 6, 1985

Why I love Chico, cont'd: That great town is having its first annual International Culture Festival March 21-22 at the fairgrounds, featuring, among other splendid events, the first annual Velveeta Cheese Cookoff.

MARCH 11, 1987

Velveeta

ONLY IN HILLSBOROUGH DEPT.

We have Jr. Leaguer Melanie Davis and Bohemian Clubber T.J. Ryan III, who had a bridle shower at Bull's Texas Cafe on Van Ness Sat. night. That "bridle" bit is not a typo. The only wedding gifts they want are for their horses! They'll be married April 28 at St. Catherine's, with a reception at the B'lingame Country Club.

APRIL 2, 1990

YESSSS, Hillsborough is different. Ronald Cameron, who lives on Marlborough Road there, rec'd a questionnaire from the town govt. about the advisability of cable TV service and relaxing satellite restrictions. Among the questions: "How many of your TV sets are for members of your live-in staff?" "Does your staff live in your primary residence or in a separate building on your property?" "How many live-in staff members do you have?" (among the choices: "Eight or more"). Ron threw the questionnaire away for fear it would fall into the hands of "my upstairs gardeners who have been griping ever since I let one of the day-shift chauffeurs use the dessert chef's sauna."

MAY 18, 1987

Yes, Hillsborough is indeed an elegant community. The other day Lucius Beebe phoned the City Hall to inquire about trash disposal, and discovered no such agency exists. "In Hillsborough," a voice informed him coldly, "most people have their gardeners remove their trash."

FEBRUARY 22, 1960

TO THE NORTH

Well, poor Marin. Marvelous Marin. Rich Marin. Concerned residents rightly resent my "Only in Marin" items, the BMW jokes, the intimations of spoiled-brattism. "We have problems just like everybody else," they write, and so here's something a bit more earthy and folksy. The Little League season in Ross Valley just ended, and Jeff Pelline says it was wonderful: Huey Lewis was a coach, the "delicious" hot dogs cost only $1.75, the fans passed around Neiman-Marcus popcorn and one of the team's cheers went like this: "We got money, we got stocks, don't need no credit cards to clean your clocks!" If not only in Marin, where?

JUNE 14, 1995

This is no time for tacky cries of "Only in Marin!" Nevertheless, it's a fact that the 12 Marin Day Schools are honoring the late Jerry Garcia by tie-dyeing shirts, socks, pants, sheets and pillowcases today, Monday and Tuesday. Jerry donated valuable Grateful Dead memorabilia each year to the schools' fund-raisers.

AUGUST 11, 1995

Maroon County on Tues. night, Mill Valley's downtown was ablaze with lights and restaurants were filled by 6 p.m. with all those people who had no water, phones, or electricity in their homes. "This is how Mill Valley responds to a natural disaster," observed Nancy Klasky. "They go out to dinner at D'Angelo's."

DECEMBER 14, 1995

ONWARD

You think the Piedmontese have problems? Try this one, in the Monterey County Sheriff's log, datelined Pebble Beach: "Despondent over a dead pet, a woman consumed an excess of Dom Perignon and medication and had to be transported to Community Hospital." That is so Pebble Beach!

SEPTEMBER 9, 1994

ITEMS IN THE ASHES OF THE EAST BAY

S.F. Fire Dept. engine No. 13, with six firefighters aboard, returning to S.F. after fighting the flames for 14 hours, was stopped at the Bay Bridge toll plaza by a collector who demanded the $1 toll. The receipt is being framed for the fire house wall.

OCTOBER 29, 1991

* * *

Berkeley architect Bill Corlett judged a contest for model homes designed by sixth-graders in Moraga and laughed later to Virginia Leach: "Some of them had left out a garage or even closets but ALL of them had swimming pools."

MAY 18, 1987

Bitter Pill: Well, Oakland is in the big leagues now —via a pro football team —and I wonder what Ambrose Bitter Bierce would have had to say about THAT. It was Bierce, I believe, who was gazing across the bay the day after the '06 fire and quake when a friend commented, "It looks like nothing happened to Oakland." Bierce nodded. "There are some things," he murmured, "that even the earth can't swallow."

FEBRUARY 2, 1960

* * *

Carrie (Princess Leia) Fisher, bride of Paul Simon, came onstage during the Simon & Garfunkel reunion at the Oak. Coliseum Sat. to beam to the crowd, "Nice to be spending our honeymoon with all of you." Interjected Paul: "Can you imagine spending your honeymoon in Oakland?" . . . Poor Oakland: So far from perfection, so near to San Francisco.

JANUARY 2, 1984

Everybody keeps asking, "What'll we do with Alcatraz?" And naturally, George Lamont has the answer: "Let's put Oakland on it," he whispers, "and then we can have the Bay Bridge all to ourselves."

JULY 8, 1965

Glitterati

"There are more of them than there are of us..."

Scenes With Hitch

On Monday afternoon the portly figure of Mr. Alfred Hitchcock was to be seen emerging, with a definite "thwuck," from a large black limousine on Powell. He waddled over to a bench in Union Square and spread himself out like a roly-poly pudding. Some nut with a paper bag sprinkled grain at his feet, attracting pigeons by the hundreds.

Kicking at them good-naturedly, the director of "The Birds" admonished: "Get thee to Ernie's — I'll see you under glass at 7."

A cunning little blonde girl, dressed in blue and shoved from behind by an elderly lady, approached him. "There he is," said the lady, "the man you see on TV." The little girl burst into tears, and Mr. Hitchcock made a face at her. "That's right, dearie," he said. "I'm the bogey man."

As the pigeons fluttered about our heads and shoulders, we talked about "The Birds," which Mr. Hitchcock described as "a fowl epic, if I ever made one. Biggest cast of extras I ever had, too. Over 28,000 birds. Of course, they all worked for chicken-feed, except for the buzzards, which had agents." ... "The ads," I said, "quote you as calling it 'the most terrifying picture I have ever made.' Is that true?"

"Oh, indubitably," he replied. "I financed it myself, and I'm terrified at the thought of losing all my money." He batted a pigeon off his bald head. "Very dirty birds," he mumbled. "Spread disease. It's a little-known fact that you can even get rabies from a pigeon."

Herb lunches at Jack's with Alfred Hitchcock in 1951.

Herbert the Furrier walked up and greeted the director. "I understand that 'The Birds' is for adults only." When Mr. Hitchcock looked blank, Herbert cackled: "No mynahs allowed!" As Mr. Hitchcock was digesting this, one Herb Ligier cut in: "They tell me you're a bear for detail. I hear you left no tern unstoned." Mr. Hitchcock sprinkled a little grain among the pigeons. "They're not so bad after all," he decided.

The Union Square character who walks around with a sandwich board reading "Eat No Pork or Fats!" arrived. Patting his stomach, Mr. Hitchcock growled: "I didn't come here to be insulted. Why, on June 1, Santa Clara University is giving me an honorary degree in the humanities. I was hoping for ornithology, of course. You see, I went to a Jesuit school and I live nearby in the Santa Cruz mountains. Perhaps some day I will be known as the Birdman of Santa Cruz."

He got up to leave, picking his way daintily through the pigeons. "Forget what I said about pigeons giving you rabies," he smiled roguishly, "unless you start foaming at the mouth in a day or two, of course." With another "thwuck," he squeezed back into the limousine, on the rear of which was a sticker reading, "'The Birds' Is Coming."

"So long," he waved. "I are going."

. . .

Add Infinitems

At the $125-a-head Police Dept. fund-raiser at the Hilton on April 9, Commsr. Lou Giraudo will present Clint Eastwood with a real inspector's star — 2211 — to replace the one he threw into the bay in disgust at the end of "Magnum Force."

APRIL 1, 1988

Page 51: Merv Griffin, Eva Gabor, and Herb at the black-tie dinner party honoring his 75th birthday in April 1991.

Marilyn and Joe

The newsboy at Columbus and B'way, an old pal of Joe DiMaggio's, shouting the headlines thisaway: "Best Man Weds Marilyn!"

JANUARY 15, 1954

Marilyn Monroe and Joe DiMaggio kiss at San Francisco City Hall on their wedding day, January 14, 1954. Tour guides to this day point out Saints Peter and Paul Church in North Beach as the site where the two were married. In fact, DiMaggio married his first wife, Dorothy Arnold, at the church in 1939 — but he married Monroe at City Hall.

John Wayne and his
wife (in lei) hold
court in one of the
exotic rooms at
Trader Vic's in
Emeryville in 1948.

Trader Vic's

When the Bay Bridge was completed,
we Loyal Sons of Hinky Dink enthused
"Hey, they built this thing just so we
could get to Vic's 20 minutes faster!"
Hinky Dink's was the original name of
Vic's, derived from the World War I
song, "Mademoiselle from Armentieres
(Hinky-Dinky Parlay-Voo)." When the
World's Fair opened on Treasure Island
in '39, Vic's became not only famous but
crowded. Even we Loyal Sons had to
wait at the bar but it was worth it. By
this time he had invented rum drinks
with gardenias, orchids and crazy
names like Missionary's Downfall and
Sufferin' Bastard. In the foyer was a
case containing two shrunken heads. It
was I who had printed the caption that
was affixed beneath them: "My, that
certainly WAS a dry martini!"

OCTOBER 11, 1984

Johnny and Helen Kan opened their restaurant in the 1950s. It was one
of the most famous restaurants in Chinatown (the other class restaurant
was Tommy Toy's Imperial Palace on Grant, now on Montgomery).
Herb regularly chronicled the famous people who made Kan's their
favorite Chinese restaurant in SF — Cary Grant, Rudolf Friml, Phil Harris
and Alice Faye. Actor Danny Kaye, also a gourmet chef, was a regular,
cooking meals with Johnny several times a year.

A favorite story of Shirley Temple Black's, at right with Matt Kelly, was the item Herb ran often about one of his cherished possessions: a blue glass pitcher bearing her likeness as a 'darlin'' child, which he used to mix martinis with this foolproof formula: 'Gin to the chin, vermouth to the tooth.'

Rabbit Test

Matt Kelly, vacationing in Marrakesh, struck up a conversation with a venerable titled Britisher – an earl, no less – who reminisced: "I was in San Francisco only once – years ago, to make a speech – and struck up a friendship with a lovely lady from Burlingame. Her husband was away on a longish trip and, well, one thing led to another. Then it became a bit sticky. She was overdue, her husband was due home any minute, and she went to take a rabbit test. Let me tell you we were both quite worried. The day after the test, I still hadn't heard from her and didn't dare call, what with her husband being home. I dined alone at the Mark Hopkins, very depressed, and as I entered my room, I heard a strange rustling noise from the bed. I turned on the light and there in the middle of the bed sat a big, white, very lively rabbit, with a pink ribbon around its neck and a note saying 'Relax, darling.' I must say, old boy, it was the classiest thing that has ever happened to me."

JUNE 14, 1975

Games People Play

Shirley Temple Black attended a United Nations Conference on Human Environment in Geneva — where, during one session, a member of the Russian delegation suddenly turned to her and remarked, "My two favorite film stars are Ginger Rogers and Shirley Temple." "Why thank you," said Shirley, smiling, at which the Russian asked, "Where is Ginger Rogers?" "She keeps busy," replied Shirley, "doing movies and television." "And," continued the Russian, "whatever happened to Shirley Temple?"

FEBRUARY 17, 1995

It was late on a Friday afternoon in October 1977. The wire services were heavy with accounts of Bing's death and with lengthy obituaries but lacking in proper personal appreciation of America's entertainment icon.

I felt such a memoir had to be the centerpiece for our page one, so once again sought out Caen to save the day.

Herb had already written his column for Monday and had headed down early for a weekend at John Gardiner's Tennis Ranch in Carmel Valley.

A very irritated Caen came to the phone (our operator said it was a news emergency) grumbling that he had hoped to finish a set of tennis before martini time, that he really never knew Crosby well, that there was no source material available to him down there and that the score was 6-all and he had to get back on the court.

I said simply there was only an hour left before the first edition deadline.

He called back 45 minutes later and dictated a 1500-word personal appreciation of Bing the man and the entertainer, which was by far the best of anything I had seen. As always it was word perfect. We featured it on page one and jumped it to a half page inside.

— BILL GERMAN, *Managing Editor*

Herb first met Bob Hope in 1936 and they remained friends throughout Herb's life. The last time they met was on the Queen Elizabeth II in 1994 en route from England to Normandy to celebrate the 50th anniversary of D-Day: 'The last of the great war entertainers, Bob Hope, performed aboard the Queen Elizabeth II last night and who is to say it wasn't his last night in such a setting? He is, after all, 91, and as gallant as they come.'

Sing, Sing, Sing

I sat back and stared at a double photograph on my office wall. The top photo shows Benny, Jerry Bundsen (my longtime aide, now retired) and me in 1937. The picture was taken one afternoon in Oakland, a few hours before the Goodman band was about to break all records at Sweet's Ballroom. Benny is standing there, wearing a sport shirt and slacks and that trademark crooked smile, his arms folded across his chest. Jerry and I are looking awed, which we were. . . . The second half of the photo was taken 35 years later, in 1972, when Benny played at Concord with a small group. We recreated the pose — Benny in the center, his arms folded across his chest, the smile still crooked. Jerry had put on a little weight and I had lost 20 pounds of hair, but the feeling is the same as it was in 1937, a feeling of love and admiration for a guy who was a factor in our lives, and the lives of so many, for 50 years or more, depending on when you first picked up on BG.

JUNE 14, 1986

I remember so many things about those great days with Herb; once I was driving my new Cadillac convertible and for some reason I was all dolled up with a white scarf and a camel hair coat, and I happened to whiz by Herb, who was walking along the sidewalk with the jockey Billy Pearson, and Billy took one look and me and said: "Herbie, do you ever get the feeling that some of the payola isn't getting through?"

Another time Herb and I were having lunch at the Garden Court of the Palace Hotel and the oh-so-elegant supercilious Mr. Lucius Beebe strode by and without missing a stride he commented out of the side of his mouth: "Eating with the *help*?"

— JERRY BUNDSEN

Jack Teagarden on trombone, Barney
Bigard on clarinet and Arvell Shaw on bass
at the Hangover Club in January 1951.

During the Korean War, André Previn was a soldier in the Army stationed in San Francisco, but was also musical director for MGM. One night he wandered into Fack's, a Market Street nightclub owned by George Andros (shown above with singer Billy Eckstine in 1948). The piano player was taking a break, and Previn asked if he could sit in for a few minutes. Sure. Herb was there. Andros was so impressed by Previn's playing, he offered him a $100 bill every time he could get away and play his own set. Previn said sure thing. When Andros told Herb about the deal, Herb said, 'Are you nuts! He makes $2,000 a week at MGM!' Said Andros: 'Gee, maybe I should have offered $150.'

Comedian Steve Allen and Herb at Mai Tai Sing's Rickshaw Lounge in 1961.

Turk Murphy

A great San Francisco name, right up there with Lefty O'Doul, Sunny Jim and Billy Ralston. A terrific guy, soft-spoken, gentlemanly, kind; I never heard him swear or lose his temper except maybe at thickheads who called his music "Dixieland" or requested "When the Saints Go Marching In," a number he detested to his dying day, I'm sure. He played New Orleans jazz, happy jazz, Frisco jazz, every number burnished to perfection, bouncing right along with the most infectious of beats.

JUNE 2, 1987

Earthquake McGoon's, above, at the foot of Market Street, was the home of the Turk Murphy Jazz Band in 1979.

At left, Herb presents an award to pianist Peter Clute and band leader Turk Murphy for their cable car decorations during 1973's '100 Years in the Groove' celebration of the 100th anniversary of the city's cable cars, an event presided over by Mayor Joe Alioto.

Santa Cause

Phyllis Diller beefing to
Merv Griffin about her ex-husband:
"He's so cheap that on Christmas
Eve, he puts the kids to bed, goes
outside, fires a shot and tells 'em
Santa Claus killed himself."

DECEMBER 1958

Phyllis Diller with San Francisco Mayor George
Christopher, Carey Baldwin and Cyril Magnin at
Noah's Ark on Fisherman's Wharf in July of 1959.

In the late '50s, when I played the Purple Onion, that popular bistro on Columbus Avenue, I was told: "If you can get Herb Caen's attention you've got it made."

When he first came in to see my act I got him in a pleasingly playful half-Nelson and whispered in his ear, "I'll sleep with you 18 times if you'll give me a good review."

He blanched, crumpled and when he regained consciousness he rasped in a frail frightened throaty groan, "Never mind. Just tell me what you want me to say."

From that day on, he gave me very valuable verbiage, amazingly adorable adjectives, special spiffy space and kindly cute kudos, all because of his fantastic phobic fear of my thrilling threat!

— PHYLLIS DILLER

Barnaby Conrad presides over his El Matador club, at left, and shares a drink at the bar with actor Tyrone Power, below, in 1959.

Dotted Line

It's hard to walk along Broadway without going all gooey over what a great street it was. Vanessi's serving great crusty burgers till 3 a.m., Barnaby Conrad's El Matador with its glamorous crowds, and next to that, Lenny Bruce at the top of his form at Ann's 440. Down the street at Montgy., Basin Street West, now a filthy eyesore, long-closed and decaying, but once the setting for Ike and Tina Turner's unforgettable 2 a.m. "breakfast" shows. And who was the opening act for the Kingston Trio at the hungry i? All of you who yelled, "Bill Cosby!" will be admitted to the Jazz Workshop for the Mastersounds' 4 a.m. jam session, featuring Wes Montgomery. Damn.

AUGUST 3, 1993

Confession

Comedian Lenny Bruce, who opened last night at Ann's 440 on B'way, confides: "I'm just like everybody else. I want to be a nonconformist, too!"

APRIL 2, 1948

Herb was one of Bruce's staunchest early supporters in the mid-'50s, when he wrote: "They call Lenny Bruce a sick comic — and sick he is. Sick of the pretentious phoniness of a generation that makes his vicious humor meaningful. He is a rebel, but not without a cause, for there are shirts that need unstuffing, egos that need deflating and precious few people to do the sticky job with talent and style. Sometimes you feel a twinge of guilt for laughing at one of Lenny's mordant jabs, but that disappears a second later when your inner voice tells you, with pleased surprise, 'But that's true.' The kind of truth that might not have dawned on you if there weren't a few Lenny Bruces around to hammer it home."

Francis Ford Coppola, Enrico Banducci, and Charlotte Mailliard Swig at the reopening of Enrico's in North Beach June 22, 1992.

Lunch With the Professor

AUGUST 12, 1965

It was the occasion of the first visit to San Francisco of Professor Marshall McLuhan, director of the Center for Culture and Technology at the University of Toronto, author of "The Mechanical Bride," "The Gutenberg Galaxy," "Understanding Media," and "The Medium Is the Message," darling of the critics ("Compared to McLuhan, Spengler is cautious and Toynbee is positively pedantic" — New York Herald-Tribune), the man who stands "at the frontier of post-Einsteinian mythologies."

Hot on the trail of this titan, I thought to myself, "Where is the last place in town you'd expect to see Marshall McLuhan?" and that's where I found him — at Off-Broadway in North Beach, lunching amid topless waitresses with writer Tom Wolfe, adman Howard Gossage, and Dr. Gerald Feigen.

Being President of the Leg Men of America, I never felt a primal urge to lunch among the topless ladies, but in such distinguished company, who could resist? "Strip steak sandwich," I said to waitress Marilyn, who was wearing blue sequin pasties and not much else. As she walked sternly away, I commented, "A good-looking girl."

"Interesting choice of words," mused Dr. McLuhan. "Good-looking girl. The remark of a man who is visually oriented, not tactually. And I further noticed that you

could not bring yourself to look at her breasts as she took your order. You examined her only after she walked away — another example of the visual: The farther she walked away, the more attractive she became."

"Actually," I apologized, blushing, "I'm rather inhibited." The professor nodded. "Another interesting word. Inhibited is the opposite of exhibited," he pointed out, "and what is exhibited causes you to be inhibited."

A topless fashion show ensued, commentated by a young lady who was fully dressed and in good voice. "Now here, gentlemen," she said, "is the ideal opera gown for your wife." A gorgeously endowed blonde appeared in a full-length gown open to the waist. The audience, composed mainly of Tuesday Downtown Operator-like types, gaped silently. "You're all dead out there," chided the commentator. "Where's the applause?"

"Now the word applause," interjected Dr. McLuhan, "comes of course from the Latin *applaudere*, which means to explode. In early times, audiences applauded to show their disfavor – they clapped their hands literally to explode the performer off the stage. Hence you might say that the silence here is a form of approbation, at least in the classical sense."

The show over, Tom Wolfe asked waitress Marilyn, "Why do you wear pasties?" "Have to," she dimpled. "It's the law, when food is being served. For health reasons, you see?" Nobody saw. We invited Marilyn and Rochelle to join us for a drink. "Before we can sit with customers," said Marilyn, "we have to put brassieres on." She and Rochelle left and reappeared wearing black bras.

"I think brassieres look sexier than pasties, don't you?" Marilyn inquired. Everybody nodded. "Besides, you can walk

Herb with Carol Doda in 1965. The two had a great relationship despite the fact that he zinged her in the early 1970s for getting new silicone injections that brought her chest measurement to 44 inches, which he said matched her age. Upon hearing in 1966 that silicone tends to migrate in the body, Herb conjectured that Doda might end up with the flattest chest and biggest nose in North Beach. So the good-natured Doda showed up at New Joe's wearing a huge plastic nose. Opposite, a pre-silicone Carol Doda dresses as 1962's New Year's baby.

faster with a brassiere." Everybody looked blank. "What I mean is," she went on, "you don't jiggle so." The discussion switched to the recent police raids on Off-Broadway, and Rochelle said, "I guess it was just a test case, we haven't been bothered since." "I see," said Dr. McLuhan. "To mix a metaphor, it was the thin edge of the trial balloon." I'm sorry to report this, but it's fact that he tittered at his own remark.

We walked out into the sunshine, to find a young man on the sidewalk, handing out blue pamphlets for the "Scandinavian Massage Studio, Miss Ingrid, Director." The copy read, "Six young and trained Scandinavian girls are ready to serve you. For the tired executive we offer private massage room, private telephones, stock quotations, the Wall Street Journal, music."

It didn't sound relaxing at all. Not half as relaxing as lunch among the nymphs with Dr. Marshall McLuhan and his merry men.

Dottering On

Tom Rooney points out that the retrospectives inspired by Frank Sinatra's 80th birthday have turned up an oddity — Frank's little-known recording of "I Left My Heart in San Francisco." He made it on Aug. 27, 1962, but withdrew it, dissatisfied, two weeks later. Tony Bennett, well-satisfied, as are we all, recorded his spellbinder Jan. 28, 1962.

DECEMBER 15, 1995

Herb loved to tweak Bennett about his 'gorgeously toupee'd' presence and referred to 'I Left My Heart in San Francisco' as the first organ transplant song, but he genuinely liked Bennett's singing and plugged every show he ever did in San Francisco. One event was a concert Bennett did in the 1970s for Friedel Klussman, the woman who mounted a long and ultimately successful campaign to save the cable cars from extinction.

Herb and Dizzy were friends for decades. Jazz loomed large in San Francisco in the '50s and '60s when the Jazz Workshop, Basin Street West, Blackhawk, Jimbo's Bop City and other clubs were hot. It wasn't unusual for the Jefferson Airplane to open for Gillespie's big band, in the mix of musical styles then common in the city. Herb recalled that he and Gillespie walked through Union Square together in those days and Dizzy had said, 'What a town, you even got a union for squares!'

Carol Channing takes theatrical producer Carole Shorenstein Hays under her wing at the 1991 San Francisco Opera opening.

Dolly Good

If you can listen to Carol Channing singing "Hello, Dolly!" at the Venetian Room without experiencing a slight lump in your throat and a fogged eye, you've got a harder heart than mine. That's showbiz history. Another reason you have to love CC even if you didn't go to Lowell: She's one funny dame.

FEBRUARY 4, 1988

Cabaret Tunes

The F'mont's Venetian Room, once "owned" by Nat King Cole, Lena Horne and Ella Fitz, is now the property of Joel Grey, who opened Tues. night to a standing ovation (among the standees: Carol Channing, Charles Lowe and Cyril Magnin, the last of whom had the gumption and poise to sit alone at a ringside table). Joel's show is the same and yet better, tighter and with more texture, and the "Cabaret" finale now seems even more eerie, with its evocation of Weimar and the Nazis. Joel does not leave 'em laughing, and good for him.

MAY 1, 1986

. . .

Melvin Belli provided great copy for years, with his many marriages, flamboyant style both in and out of the courtroom, and disregard for the traditional wooing of the press. When he took his 'third and a half' wife, Pat Montandon, in 1966, in a Shinto ceremony in Japan, the marriage lasted just 36 days. Herb described the debacle as '30 seconds over Tokyo.'

Above, celebrity waiters Melvin Belli and Willie McCovey offer Cyril Magnin a glass of wine during a 1984 fund-raiser. At right, Belli and Pat Montandon arrive at San Francisco International Airport In 1966.

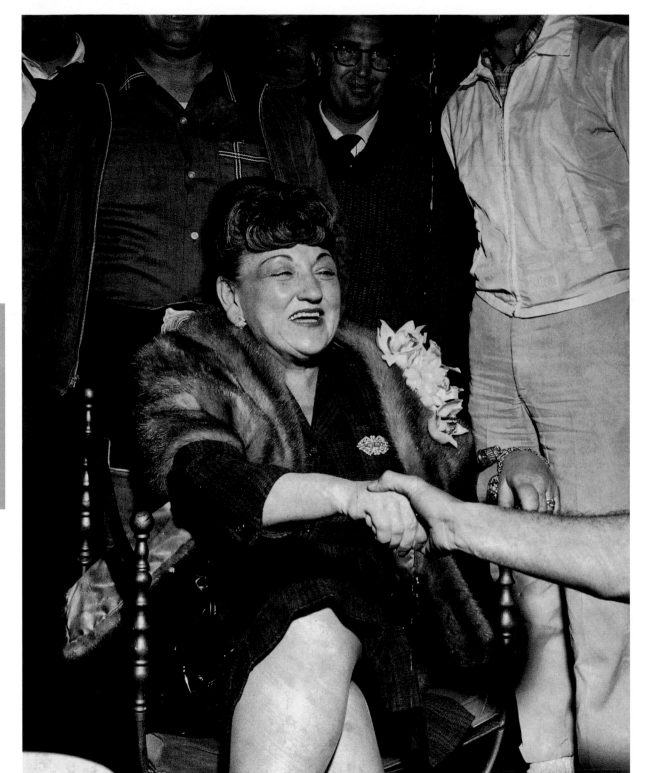

Madam Stanford

Sally Stanford is off tomorrow for a month in Europe. "Have you ever been abroad?" she was asked. "Always," she replied tartly.

OCTOBER 9, 1962

Famed madam
Sally Stanford
in April 1962.

Scott Beach, foreground, and Michael McCourt at Perry's on Union Street in 1989.

Inside Out

Michael McCourt, the celebrity bartender, may have saved renaissance man Scott Beach's life a few nights ago. During a dinner party at the Mansion Hotel, Scott began choking on a piece of meat, whereupon he poked Michael, and pointed at his throat. "I didn't pay much attention at first," recalls McCourt. "His face was contorted, so I thought he was doing an imitation of "The Phantom of the Opera." Then, realizing at last that Beach was in real trouble, he leaped behind him and expertly applied the Heimlich maneuver. When Scott recovered his breath and poise, he hugged McCourt and asked, "Was it good for you, too?"

FEBRUARY 1, 1988

Big Joe Alioto

Big Joe won't be amused, but it sounded funny at the Washbag when Michael McCourt said, "Angela won despite the name recognition."

NOVEMBER 6, 1992

Cartoonist Charles Schulz with Snoopy character and Mayor Alioto in 1968.

Bay City Beat

It looked like old times last wk. on Union, where Perry's was celebrating its 20th annivy. by rolling back beer and wine prices to 1969 (four-bits and six-bits, which still sounds like enough). As a result, there were lines out to the gutters and beautiful and not-so-beautiful bodies stacked six deep around the bar, where celebrity bartenders got in the way of the old pros, Michael McCourt, Michael Fogarty and Paul McManus. Thurs. night was a mob scene multiplied, with people hollering for service and autographs from Huey Lewis, Willie Brown, Randy Cross and Dwight Clark, none of whom was able to produce more than foam from the beer tap. Funniest sightem: Wee Willie Brown trying to pick up a long-haired beauty, unaware that she's huge Randy Cross' lady friend. All the tips, by the way, went to the Special Olympics, and they were sizable.

AUGUST 21, 1989

Dwight Clark, Willie Brown, Herb and Huey Lewis at Perry's 20th Anniversary in 1989.

Math Riddle

Wilkes Bashford revealed the Willie Brown formula for dating: "As he gets older, his dates get younger. That's because the total of Willie's age and the age of his date must never exceed 100."

MARCH 26, 1996

Election of the Century

Yes, once more into the polls, dear friend. On the face of it, tomorrow's Election of the Century, not to be confused with the trial of the same name, should be a no-brainer. Willie Brown is in a class by himself — and a bargain by any standard: For a piddling $137,000 a year, we have the chance to get a $1 million-a-year superstar. Not only that, he'll work 24 hours a day, seven days a week because the man is an insomniac. As politics is his life, San Francisco is his love and he'll be burning the midnight oil at noon and vice versa. If elected, Willie Brown will be all over the place, shaking hands, turning on the charm, listening carefully to your problems (he has impeccable manners) and trying to solve them.

NOVEMBER 6, 1995

Future mayor Willie Brown models leather
pants and cowboy boots at a
Wilkes Bashford fashion show in 1978.

The Impressario

Fillmore Bill Graham's plan to take a show of top rockers to So. Vietnam is looking rockier by the minute. The Defense Dept. won't clear any groups that have been busted for pot or appeared at anti-war rallies — and that takes care of just about everybody except Lawrence Welk, who is not what the troops are crying for.

SEPTEMBER 3, 1970

Showbiz Saga

Yesterday we told you how a very young and unknown Robin Williams auditioned for a job with The Tubes — that was on Aug.1, 1976 — only to be turned down by the chief judge, then-famous Martin Mull. Well, Marilyn Woods, who was doing some work for The Tubes at the time, has a videotape of the audition and it's historic. Robin, working at the time as a dishwasher at The Trident in Sausalito while struggling as a comic, walked in bowlegged wearing a cowboy hat, no shirt over his furry chest, and furry chaps and boots. He launched into an original song called "Hormone Blues" that began "Went to bed last night with hair on my chest, woke up this mornin' with two lovely breasts — hey, I'm changin'! I've got those hormone bluuuuues," at which point Mull cuts him off with a "Thank you, Number 27". . . . By the way, it seems Martin Mull isn't as unknown now as he was famous then. Irate fans remind me he's a regular on "Roseanne" but Mr. Nite Life does not stay home and watch TV.

DECEMBER 2, 1993

Comedian and actor Robin Williams lurking in a doorway during a 1987 interview. Rock promoter Bill Graham in his office in 1984, opposite page.

Herb was a good friend of artist Beniamino Bufano, shown above in 1945 and at right in front of the 1966 restoration of the Palace of Fine Arts. Bufano had come to San Francisco 14 years before Herb and was well established in North Beach as an artist and character when Herb began the column. He chronicled Bufano's lively disputes with patrons, landlords, friends and detractors. His favorite Bufano sculptures were the stainless steel statue of Sun Yat-sen in St. Mary's Square and the powerful St. Francis at City College, made of melted-down handguns Bufano collected after the assassination of John F. Kennedy.

Mr. San Francisco's Genesis

I've been living here, man and boy,
since nine months before I was born,
having been conceived during the
1915 Panama Pacific Int'l Exposition
on what became the Marina.
(No, my parents were not in a sideshow;
they merely spent the summer here,
complaining about the cold.)

JUNE 14, 1996

Deadlinitis

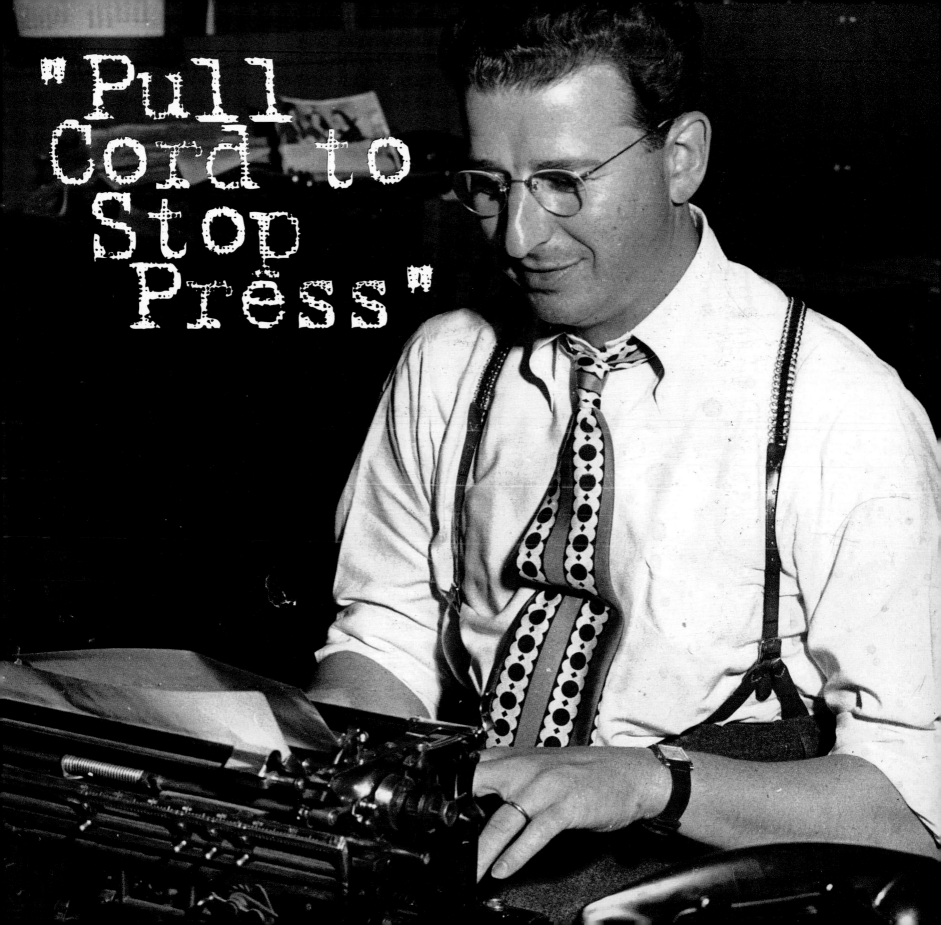

"Pull Cord to Stop Press"

My Remarkable Career

I never complain about paying my taxes. The government spent plenty on me during World War II and didn't come close to getting its money's worth. The military didn't know what to do with me. Shortly after Pearl Harbor, I volunteered for the Marines. One Colonel West, an irascible recruiter, found me deaf, dumb and blind.

I was disappointed, but he did me a favor. Island-hopping was no picnic. Then I volunteered for Navy officer training and was rejected for "tachycardia" (uneven heartbeat, not a tacky heart, necessarily). After the war, a nice local doctor wrote to tell me my heart was just fine. "It was your guts," he explained. "Our commanding officer hated yours." So I decided to wait to be drafted, which didn't take long. The head of my draft board was A.A. Tiscornia, an eccentric real estater who owned a row of eyesore buildings on Kearny that I lambasted regularly.

At Monterey Presidio I made two vows: I would never volunteer and I would never work in public relations, the lowest of the military low. The Army barber gave me my first "white sidewalls" haircut. My first wife, Bea, who apparently had married me for my naturally curly hair, burst into tears. So did I. I took a mechanical aptitude test and got a high score, which came as a shock since I can't open a can of soup without cutting myself. I was classified a "radio operator/ mechanic." German war bonds rose to a new high. I was shipped off to Sheppard Field near El Paso, Texas, a hellhole. I also discovered I was in the Army Air Force. We learned to sing "Off we go into the wild blue yonder," with special humorous emphasis on "We go up to fame or go down in flame." I met a lot of Southern boys who cursed continuously and vividly.

I was shipped off to Chicago to learn the Morse code, 25 words a minute. New classification: "Radio operator/gunner." Grrrr. The extravagant Air Force had commandeered the then-largest hotel in the world, the 3,000-room Stevens. We were six to a room and we cleaned the bathroom with toothbrushes. For some reason to do with brown-nosing, I was put in charge of marching the troops to the Morse code place. "Hup-two-threep-fo'!" I sang out as we marched down Michigan Ave. I discovered I had an unsuspected and unwelcome streak of

Still extravagant, the Air Force had taken over most of the big houses on Philadelphia's "Main Line." Again we had to scour the hell out of latrines, but anal-retentive is still better than whatever's the opposite. Then off to Yale for a crash course in communications and a 2nd Lieutenant's gold bars. It's a custom to give $5 to the first enlisted man to salute you. Privates Broderick Crawford and Tony Martin were waiting for me.

First shavetail assignment: communications officer of the 113th Tactical Reconnaissance Squadron, a National Guard outfit out of Indianapolis. We were stationed at Alamo Field in San Antonio, Texas. Then we were moved to Abilene, a dry town with booze available anywhere.

chickenbleep. I had those guys counting cadences, doing flankers and singing "I've Got Sixpence." We got so good that our picture appeared in the Chicago Tribune. The guys hated my guts anyway and rightly.

I barely made 25 words a minute in Morse and flunked the gunnery exam. Poor depth perception, the columnists' occupational hazard. But God bless Hap Arnold, chief of the Army Air Force! Hap was set on a separate Air Force, eventually, so he was dumping the Army Signal Corps for his own communications (this was summer of '42). I became an Air Force Cadet (hot-looking prop on cap) and shipped off to the Valley Forge Military Academy in Wayne, Pa., for officer training.

Our pilots were flying P-39s, Bell Aircobras, a pretty plane with a tendency to return unexpectedly to earth at high speed. We lost a lot of lovely guys. As communications officer, I survived periodic inspections because the old Guard sergeants covered my ass. I learned early that it would be a sergeant's war, and it was. I also liked the Air Force's informality — everybody on a first-name basis, especially if you had a seven-letter name starting with "a." We were transferred to Alexandria, La., for maneuvers with the infantry. It rained a lot and we slept in the mud under the wings of our hated P-39s.

Things moving fast now. Out went the P-39s, in came the P-38 Lightnings. The pilots loved them except when they

bailed out and hit the twin tails. "Listen to those engines," they'd say. "Sound like Cadillacs!" They were. We got our orders. Still secret but since we were issued tropical clothing we had a fair idea. Then — bombshell! Consternation, even. The famous old 113th Tac Recon was deactivated. Just-likethat. We hugged, kissed, cried, and had a wake at the Bentley Hotel in Alexandria. I was shipped off to an officers' replacement pool in Birmingham, Ala. "How the hell do I get overseas?" I asked an old-timer. "Volunteer for Air Force Intelligence," he said. "You'll be on the next ship." In Harrisburg, Pa., I became an aerial photo interpreter. I had volunteered for the first time, but I still wasn't a damned public relations officer.

One midnight we shipped out on the Ile de France. In England, I sat in a muddy camp, awaiting assignment to a squadron. I was summoned to headquarters and handed orders to report to Air Force headquarters, code name "Wide Wing." An officer there had recognized my name on the list of new arrivals. My new classification: Public relations officer. And that's why I pay my taxes without a murmur.

On the Waterfront

[Harry Bridges] was a great guy, lean, mean and salty, with a bit of a swagger. For years, he cast a long shadow over the San Francisco waterfront, for better or worse but definitely for history. To his followers, he was a hero; to his enemies, "the man who killed the port." Either way, he was a hard-boiled original, a man of integrity, a chapter in the San Francisco legend . . . Harry fighting the bosses on the waterfront, Harry beating the government that wanted to deport him, Harry dancing the night away at La Fiesta on Bay, Harry lunching at a shocked Pacific-Union Club with a mischievous editor Paul Smith.

APRIL 2, 1990

Herb was a staunch union man and supported a variety of strikes in San Francisco, although he occasionally disagreed with some of the tactics. He marched the picket lines daily during two newspaper strikes, in 1966 and 1994. The photo at right was taken during the 1994 newspaper strike, during which Herb wrote a column for the union's strike newspaper. Labor leader Harry Bridges and sculptor Beniamino Bufano, above, at a Memorial Day rally in 1963. At far right, a standoff along the Embarcadero during the Longshoremen's strike in 1946.

Some Slump

Lee Mendelson, the talented producer of documentary films, is currently making one called "A Man Named Mays" — about Willie, of course — and during last Thursday's Giants-Mets game he had his cameras set up on the field for some action shots. As Mays came to bat in the third inning, the cameras began rolling, to a chorus of jeers from the fans, one of whom hollered: "You're wasting your time, he's in a slump." On the next pitch Willie crashed a home run, the cameras following the ball all the way to the left-field stands. "See?" screeched a Little Old Lady in a front-row box, "I told you these games are fixed!"

MAY 17, 1962

Herb shows some muscle for giant among Giants Willie Mays in 1963, below. Giants Manager Dusty Baker visits with Chris Isaak before the singer performs The National Anthem in 1994, right.

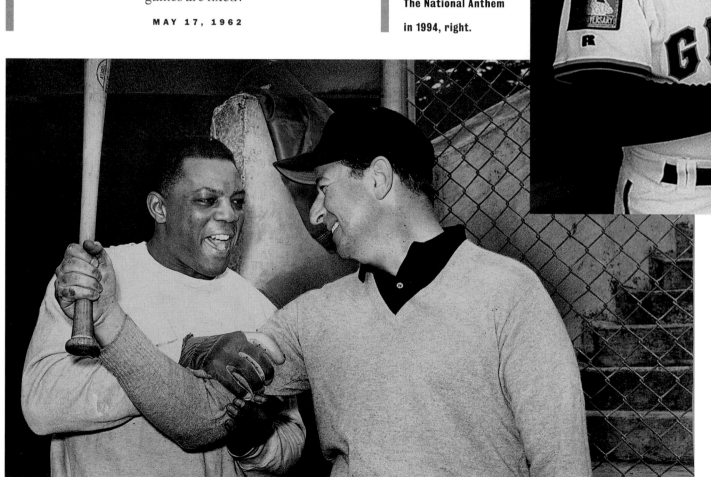

Once, while listening to a Giants game as he headed to North Beach, Caen drove into the Broadway Tunnel when the score was 4 to 2 for the Giants. When he emerged on the other side, the score was 6 to 4 and the Giants had lost. He had no idea who hit the game-winning grand slam. He lobbied for months for a wire to improve reception inside the tunnel, and finally got one donated.

Scottsdale, Arizona

Spring training! One of the nicest two-word phrases in the language, along with "check enclosed," "open bar," and "class dismissed." During spring training, the baseball world is once again starting from scratch, except maybe for the Seattle Mariners and the Atlanta Braves. Theoretically, though, everybody has a chance to go All The Way, except maybe for the Baltimore Orioles and the Texas Rangers. Theorize all you want but God is still on the side with the biggest bats, the fattest payrolls and the sweetest pitching, except for the Dodgers, who have the fattest and luckiest manager, Stomach Disorda, and Orel Hershiser, the hummmmm-baby of pitchers. Overall, though, the bodies are young and eager, the white balls rise high against the blue sky and the clichés sound new all over again. In the rickety stands, the old-timers rusticate, ruminate, masticate and occasionally expectorate, gazing sourly at the sweet birds of youth on the greenest of grass.

MARCH 14, 1989

Willie McCovey signs autographs the day he announces his retirement in June 1988.

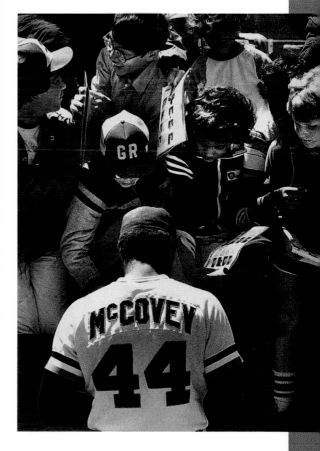

Caryl Chessman, left, who was executed in San Quentin's gas chamber in May 1960. A funeral car carries Chessman's body from San Quentin, above. Herb had witnessed executions and had become a strong death penalty opponent. Although he was a friend of Governor Pat Brown, it always rankled him that Brown didn't pardon Chessman.

A Dark and Dreadful Thing

MAY 1, 1960

At 10:00 a.m. tomorrow — while you sit at your desk or lie in your bed, while you wash your dishes or pound your typewriter, while traffic rolls along freeways and schoolchildren sit at their desks to learn about truth and justice and equality — a 39-year-old man named Caryl Whittier Chessman will go to the gas chamber in San Quentin, there to be thrown into a metal chair by nervous guards, there to be strapped in like a wild animal, there to sniff the poisonous fumes and writhe in agonized aloneness for a few eternal minutes, and then to be pronounced dead by competent medical authority.

All this to satisfy you, dear citizen, to satisfy the conscience of the sovereign State of California, to demonstrate that Society strikes down its attackers, thereby re-emerging pure and undefiled. None of these things will happen, of course. You, for whose protection this savage rite is being conducted, will feel deeply troubled or indifferent, depending on your sensibilities. The Golden State will be less golden for having plunged into the Dark Ages. And Society will be as corrupt and exposed as ever.

I have heard their voices and read their letters — the proponents of capital punishment who cry like the cold-eyed fanatics of old: "It must be done, it is written in the Bible, 'an eye for an eye.'" There is also something in the Bible about turning the other cheek, but no matter. Neither argument is tenable.

The man, Caryl Chessman, is no longer the issue; now he is the worldwide symbol of the farce that is capital punishment. Even those who thirst for his death are no longer quite clear about his crimes, nor do they care; all they know is that he has made a mockery of the law for 12 years — thereby casting doubt into the hearts of all men — and this is inherently Bad. A man should be condemned and go quietly to his death in an orderly fashion. Consigned to the gas chamber under a hysterical new law that now seems as archaic as the Iron Maiden (his crime — 'kidnapping for robbery with bodily harm' — has been duplicated scores of times, with no talk of death penalty), he used other laws to fight a fantastic fight against fantastic odds.

"Oh, well," a man said the other night as he chewed on a filet in a fashionable restaurant. "It's not the worst way to die. It's all over in a few seconds and it's comparatively painless, they say." Not the worst way to die? Can you think of a worse way: to have the time and place scheduled for you, to be the star in a hideous sideshow before goggle-eyed witnesses, to die a meaningless death at the hands of a State seeking to cancel a crime by committing another?

I saw my first executions when I was a kid police reporter on

The Sacramento Union. Three, in fact. The State, not having yet achieved the ultimate in refinement, was hanging them then. On a hot summer day, I drove up to Folsom Prison to cover the hanging of a young man who, in the course of his first holdup, had lost his head and killed a storekeeper. I talked to him in his cell many times during the trial. He was sad, sick and scared. So was I.

"Don't worry, kid," the warden affably told me. "It's all over in a minute. Doesn't hurt a bit." I wondered how he knew.

We, the witnesses and press, stood nervously together on the cement floor of a big room, looking up at the gallows. The new rope, scientifically tested, dangled in the sunlight streaming through barred windows. Suddenly the door behind the scaffold swung open and the nightmare scene was enacted in a flash: The murderer, his arms bound, was hustled roughly onto the trapdoor, the noose was slammed around his neck, a black mask dropped over his unbelieving face, the trapdoor clanged open, the body shot through and stopped with a sickening crack. For an eternity, the victim twitched in spasm after spasm, and one by one the witnesses began fainting around me. "Doesn't hurt a bit," the warden had said.

And from that day on, having been made properly aware of the State's awful vengeance, no holdup man ever again killed a shopkeeper? You bet.

That, after all, is the purpose of capital punishment: to set an Example. And if this is so, why isn't it done properly? Why isn't Caryl Chessman gassed in the middle of Union Square at high noon, so that thousands of people (plus millions of TV viewers) can witness the fate of wrongdoers and vow, then and there, never to step outside the law? But no, that would be an indecent spectacle, abhorrent to those who prefer to live by euphemisms. He must be done away with in a gloomy little room surrounded by a protective nest of walls, before the eyes of a few select witnesses — as though the act itself, the final demonstration of the majesty of the law, were some dark and dreadful thing. And a dark and dreadful thing it is.

Capital punishment protesters angry over the execution of Caryl Chessman cross the Golden Gate Bridge in May 1960.

Beat poets assemble outside City Lights bookstore in 1965. From left, upper top row: Stella Levy, Lawrence Ferlinghetti. Second row, standing: Donald Schenker, Michael Grieg, unknown, Mike Gibbons, David Miltzer, Michael McClure, Allen Ginsberg, Dan Langton, Steve Broston, Gary Goodrow and son Homer, Richard Brautigan behind Goodrow, Andrew Hoyem on stretcher, Lee Meyerzov. Seated: Unknown, Shig Murao, Lew Welch, Peter Orlovsky.

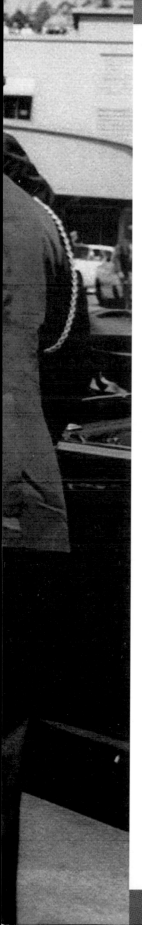

Black Friday

NOVEMBER 24, 1963

You sat by a window and stared out at the empty street, your mind still and cloudy as the skies. Odd, nagging thought: Gavin Arthur, grandson of the 21st President of the United States, had refused to vote for Jack Kennedy in 1960, although he is a Democrat. Arthur, the expert on horoscopes, had cast one whose signs, he said, indicated only one thing: The 35th President would die in office. You smiled condescendingly at him, then. There was a brief, terrible silence on the radio. And then the announcer, clearing his throat, said the simple words

"John Fitzgerald Kennedy, the 35th President of the United States, is dead." There was a brief interlude of recorded classical music that sounded like Beethoven and then the "Star-Spangled Banner" came on. The great flag on the Telephone Building was slowly lowered to half-staff, where it rippled briefly in the cold air and then sagged.

And so you cried. You cried for the young man and his wife and his family. You cried because you hadn't realized how much the young man meant to you. You cried for every stupid joke you ever listened to about him, and you cried for the fatuous faces of the people who told them. You cried for the Nation, and the despoilers of it, for the haters and the witch-hunters, the violent, the misbegotten, the deluded. You cried because all the people around you were

President John Fitzgerald Kennedy arrives at Lawrence Livermore Laboratory in March 1962.

crying, in their impotence, their frustration, their blind grief.

By early afternoon the city had collected itself slightly. The sun tried to force its way through the overcast, but it was a feeble effort. Downtown, the Salvation Army bells were ringing on the streetcorners — mournfully. A cable car rattled over distant tracks, sounding like firecrackers far away. Now the radio announcers had regained their aplomb, and a few commercials were creeping back on. One Senator said, "Words are of no use at a time like this," but other politicians had their statements prepared. A San Mateo lady I know took her son to the dentist, and said, "Isn't it terrible?" "Oh, I don't know," said the dentist. "I didn't like him or his politics." She managed to walk out into the hallway before she became ill.

The President is dead. Long live the President.

· · ·

97

Herb nicknamed actor Sterling Hayden 'Sterbo,' and visited him in Tahiti with Barnaby Conrad in 1959. Hayden moved back to Marin County in the '60s, where he lived until his death in 1986. At the time, Herb ran an obit that concluded with Hayden's own epitaph: 'Got no whales but had one hell of a fine sail.'

Tourists take a closer view of Alcatraz in 1962, before the prison was shut down.

Escape from Alcatraz

A New York newspaper hack, in town to do a Sunday supplement kind of piece about last year's Alcatraz escape, received this confidential word from a prison official: "At this point we have no alternative but to assume that all three made it."

The newsman, by the way, was entranced with this sidelight to the escape: Sterling Hayden, who lives on Belvedere, got so excited over the trio's derring-do that every night for a week he left his Volkswagen parked on the pier nearest Alcatraz (Tiburon's), with the keys in the car and peanut butter sandwiches on the seat.

DECEMBER 5, 1962

Operation Parks

The Indians are to be removed from Alcatraz. Date so far unspecified. Code name for the action is Operation Parks. It will be a Coast Guard show, with Navy participation. Landing barges will be used, but not helicopters. Staging area for invasion is Treasure Island.

At any rate, that is the way I interpret a message, marked "Confidential," dispatched Monday from the Commander of the 12th Naval District here to the commander, Western Sea Frontier, on Treasure Island. And how does the Coast Guard feel about being cast in the role of villain by the Navy? Remember Operation Custer?

SEPTEMBER 4, 1970

One of Herb's many serious
news scoops, Operation Parks
embarrassed the General
Services Administration,
the Navy, Coast Guard and
several agencies involved in
the removal of the Indians
who occupied Alcatraz in 1970.

Know It All

After watching and reading Robert Strangelove McNamara, Gloomy Dean Rusk and Maxwell Taylor, not to mention the Sage of the Pedernales, I now know all there is to know about the war in Vietnam except (1) why we are there, (2) what we're fighting for, and (3) how and when we are going to extricate ourselves. . . . The two words in their rhetoric that have become the most threadbare and meaningless: "freedom" and "aggression."

MARCH 13, 1966

S.I. Hayakawa, who was appointed acting president of San Francisco State University during the 1968 student strike and riots and later became a U.S. senator, wears his trademark tam-o-shanter during a press conference on campus.

Cracked Crystal Ball

The Hastings law college newspaper ran a series of student predictions on the outcome of the Patty Hearst trial, as follows . . . Mike Mayer: "Probably not guilty." Nancy Rassmussen: "Acquitted, because the jury will be sympathetic." Frances Rice: "Acquitted, primarily because of inequities. If she were poor and black, she'd be convicted." Mike Wood: "Guilty — six months in Hawaii."

MARCH 22, 1976

Members of an anarchist commune, above, pose for a 'family portrait' in front of their Parker Street digs in Berkeley along with some neighborhood kids in September 1971.

Retreat Into Madness

How to judge the insanity surrounding the end of Rev. Jim Jones and his strange mission? A common theme is "Who could have expected *this*?" but perhaps Götterdammerung was inevitable. Step by step, Jim Jones and his followers retreated from the comparative reality of the San Francisco ghetto to the impassable jungles, where madness could take root. Good men and women are dead — there is sorrow.

NOVEMBER 21, 1978

The Rev. Jim Jones and
the Rev. A. Ubalde, Jr.
are sworn in as housing
commissioners by
Mayor George Moscone
in November 1977.

Supervisor Dan White is taken into the Hall of Justice after his arrest in the assassinations of Moscone and Milk, November 27, 1978. Below, 'The Mayor of Castro Street,' Supervisor Harvey Milk, at the 1978 Gay Freedom Day Parade.

Horror Upon Horror, Shock Upon Shock

NOVEMBER 28, 1978

"The world has gone mad" is the phrase that sprang to people's minds and lips yesterday.

The vocabulary of grief and disbelief stretches only so far. The ghastliness of Guyana exhausted the pitifully few words at our command.

And then came the shock waves of yesterday.

The Mayor, a good man, dead. The Supervisor, a good man, dead. Their suspected killer, we had been told many times by his supporters, was a good man, too. . . .

It was all — senseless. Like the hundreds dead in Guyana. Like the young President and his brother and the great black leader . . . there must be a thread connecting all this violence. As so-called civilized people, we must be failing, somehow.

George Moscone and Harvey Milk had much in common. They were joyous men, celebrants of life, believers in people. They were eminently sane and reasonable. If they had any faults, they were those of generosity, of a willingness to think the best.

As I look out over the city that George Moscone and Harvey Milk loved, a flag is slowly being lowered to half staff. Two valuable, invaluable, irreplaceable people are dead, their families and friends grief-stricken. Hundreds are dead in Guyana, leaving tears and mystery in their wake. The phones are suddenly silent, the streets quiet. A pall settles over the holiday hills, Monday's mourning broken only by the siren that has become the sound of the city.

Warriors

Franklin Mieuli, owner of the Warriors, lunched twice at Nate Thurmond's The Beginning on Fillmore last week with 6-foot-11-inch Nate waiting on him. "Not a bad waiter," says Franklin, "but the food gets cold while he's bending down to serve it."

MARCH 14, 1973

Nate Thurmond, number 42, leaps to intercept a ball at a Warriors game in 1969. Their jerseys read "The City," and were designed personally by owner Franklin Mieuli. The team was roundly booed by New Yorkers when they played there since they thought only New York could be called "THE city."

The New Rulers of the Universe

There is a new Mr. San Francisco, plural. Move over Cyril Magnin — and make room for Bill Walsh and the 49ers, the new rulers of the universe of football and assorted galaxies. . . . I don't really know what a Super Bowl can do for a city, but San Francisco must be a different place right now. A little more joyous, a little more confident and perhaps happy to shed the title of Kook Capital of the World. Now, we have the muscles, we have the Title, we have the kind of brawling image that goes back to the real 49ers.

JANUARY 23, 1982

49er owner Eddie DeBartolo, Mayor Dianne Feinstein and 49er head coach Bill Walsh in the monster parade down Market Street on January 25, 1982, following the 49ers victory over the Cincinnati Bengals in Superbowl XVI.

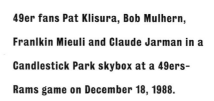

49er fans Pat Klisura, Bob Mulhern, Franlkin Mieuli and Claude Jarman in a Candlestick Park skybox at a 49ers–Rams game on December 18, 1988.

Quake, Rattle and Roll

At 5:03 p.m., Sandy Walker and I were standing in a long line for beers. A minute later, we were reeling and hanging onto each other for support. "Earthquake!" I hollered. In the crowd's sudden silence, you could hear the old concrete structure grinding away, its steel bones bending but not, thankfully, breaking. The floor rippled and shook for what seemed like 30 seconds. The terrified young women behind the beer counter stood rooted under the swaying signs. They were statues with bulging eyes, holding empty glasses. Candlestick slowly settled back into place, more or less. There was an instant babble of excited talk. The guy at the head of the line pounded on the counter and complained, "Hey, what about our beers?" His remark seemed like a return to normalcy but in retrospect, it had a surreal quality.

OCTOBER 19, 1989

A firefighter retrieved a surfboard from a Marina District home devastated by the Loma Prieta earthquake.

re you listen... "Bridges," at... TV series, "Bridges," at...
--a black woman wearing a "DA MAYOR" cap...
three chess players, saying "The one who beats me...
Why a mayoress?
...mmissioner"... Because this scene w...
...ago. "Da mayor" is played by L.A. actress Candy Br...
a stretch from Willie Brown Mineola... Willie was...
...ut said "I don't d...re" sta...sh...
Speaking of which! Jack and Anita Castor of San F...
...ue Train from Johannesburg to Capetown, were hande...
...tions, printed in English and Afrikaans, and when they c...
laughed, "Are we still in California?" (Yeah, "Dra...
... And getting back to the Geary Theater, take...
...s")... as you can get these days for a mere $...
...rd. However, the openin...
been honor...

Caenfetti

'They're off and strolling.'

Herb's journalistic career began at Sacramento High School's student newspaper, The X-Ray, where he wrote a column, sometimes called 'Corridor Gossip' and sometimes called 'Man About School' under such dubious noms de plume as Candy Caen, Hurry Caen, and Raisen Caen. The jokes weren't much better. But by the end of that year he'd developed a style that laid the groundwork for columns to come years later — a mix of gossip, puns, potpourri and human interest items as shown in these excerpts, from his June 3, 1932, column.

Herb tries to walk like a cowboy, above, during a trip to Yosemite in 1941.

Previous page: Bandleader Jerry Lester, Herb and Art Linkletter (then a radio personality in San Francisco) take part in a hobby horse race at the old Music Box night club on O'Farrell Street in 1940.

Man About School

BY HURRY CAEN

Things I never knew till now: Ruth Friedberg made a vow never to bob her hair. (Times are hard.) Bob Mallett hates turnips. (Carrots are insipid.) Helen Burdick can't stand Clark Gable. (Just to be different.) Frank Casey (Jr.) gets sore when people talk about his eyelashes. (He's always sore.) Pata Sullivan has a secret passion for Joe George. Coach E.A. Combatalade wears only bow ties and is the best-dressed teacher in school. (Just ask him.) Jackson C. Gillis uses perfume. (Breath of Roses is his favorite.) Walter Cameron has a yen to be a policeman. (He already has big feet.) Hal Burd wears only black shoes. (That's the only pair he has.) Phoebe Gorsch likes red hair. (Well dye is cheap.)

And so on. He even indulged in three-dottism when he was still in his teens:

Potpourri: Signatures reveal character, especially those appearing on school furniture. . . . teachers may have a hard time putting grades on the cards, but it is nothing compared to the trouble of explaining them after we get home. . . . to quote an eminent professor: "The test will be run on the honor system. . . . the teacher has the honor and the students have the system". . . . if we were graded on our intentions, we'd all be honor students. . . . or would we? . . . and after graduation, the sweet girl goes off to conquer the world, one man at a time. . . . stagging seems to be a habit for some and a necessity for others. . . . Lola Davey and Betty Pierce have gotten their hair cut. . . . summer is here.

HERB CAEN ON THE AIR LANES... MAURE

Nation-Wide Broadcast Of 'Samson and Delilah' Tops Today's Features

By HERB CAEN

Its importance buried beneath a load of Christmas tinsel the Metropolitan Opera radio season opened Thursday over the Nation wide NBC network.

...ately so much time was being spent wishing ... that the splendid

AIR BEAUTY ★ ★ ★ SAL

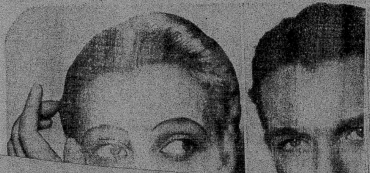

Herb C
Baghdad-

Friday Fish-Fry

THINK YOU'VE heard t
Michelsen's squabble with hi
should be so lucky. Today, A
file an appeal on the narco
Twain the most—and the o
start all over again. . . ."T
ring Marlon Brando, Montgy
(dean MARTIN???) will be
Fox tomorrow eve. . . . Harry
last wk.—second time in four
...600 block on W

It's NEWS To Me
Says Herb Caen

Personal Note
Yesterday was the Fourth ...

FINANCIAL
News of Business World
Classified Advertisements

FOUNDED 1865   CCCC

San Francisco Chronic

SAN FRANCISCO, TUESDAY, JULY 5, 1938

HERB CAEN

Ar

6D

News

FAN-ABOUT-TOWN
... by Herb Caen

BIG BUILDUP:
THEY call him Del Cari...
press ...

4

HERB CAEN
Answers His Mail

...—a fine way to talk about Mr. Farle...
house again this we

HERB CAEN

The Rambling Wreck

THERE'S MONEY in the art business, especially if you're Richard Stephens. The ebullient Mr. Ste-phens, owner of the Academy of Art College here (seven downtown campuses, 5,200 students), emerged last Fri. as the new owner of Nob Hill's celebrated "jewel box" mini-mansion — a discreet one-story fa-cade that balloons into 12 rooms as it descends the hill toward Pine. Located next to 1001 Californi... house enjoyed its golden age with ... Betty and Robert Wat... couple Mr....

Whatever Turns You On

I WAS SITTING in my third-floor office
Chron U.. staring across the street at the poli...
"Eye in the Sky" TV camera at the corner
Fifth and Mission. The camera was staring at m
I waved and the camera bobbed its head sligh...

The Swashbucklers

Columnist Stanton Delaplane, the great stylist who died last Monday, started on The Chronicle the same year I did (1936), and that started me thinking about what a helluva newspaper town this used to be. Four daily newspapers battling for circulation, each with its stable of star reporters — a colorful, hard-drinking, heavy-smoking crowd. Like their inspiration, Hildy Johnson of "The Front Page," they cursed, cheated, played around with ladies other than their wives, took incredible pride in their paper, jeered at the opposition, double-crossed their own grandmothers for a scoop and wrote damn good copy under deadline pressure. "It's a great story!" the city editor would bark, glancing at the city room clock. "Write it in takes" — a take being a short piece of copy paper — and our hero would pound it out a paragraph at a time, slugged "MTK," with a copy boy standing at his shoulder to snatch the paper out of his typewriter and run it out to the composing room. "MTK" meant "More to Kum," and there was more kumming even as the presses roared into the

"6 A.M. final" and we all went to an all-night eating joint on Powell to stare at the Page One headline and beam "Beat the hell out of 'em, didn't we?"

The young Delaplane was one of those guys who could come through like a champ on a fast-breaking story, sitting sort of sideways at the old Underwood, one leg draped over the other, a cigaret dangling from his lower lip, writing take after take of perfect copy, the sentences short and stabbing, the angle uniquely his. He was 80 years old when he died of emphysema, and he died his way, drinking his straight-up martinis and smoking to the end. "If he'd done what the docs told him to, maybe he'd still be alive," I said to a doctor. "If he'd done what they told him to," said the doc, "he'd probably have died at 75."

Delaplane and the other ace reporters made this a super newspaper town. They knew the city upside down, which it usually was, and who was getting paid off and why. They knew the madams and the shysters (the "mouthpieces") and the after-hours joints. In police parlance, they hardly ever turned anybody in — they used the shady characters for sources. The Press Club was really a Press Club, running all night and paying the bills via a bank of slot machines in the bar. An eager young D.A. named Pat Brown closed down the slot machines in the bar. "And to think we helped elect the summbitch," the newsmen growled around the bar.

Four papers, each with its constituency. The lordly Examiner, then at Third and Market, was a morning paper with a managing editor, **Bill Wren**, who "ran the town." That was his rep, and he did nothing to deny it. He chewed on cigars, mayors, police chiefs and lazy reporters. The Chronicle was safely Republican, big with the social set and financial people and famous for The Sporting Green. In the afternoon, The Call-Bulletin had a pink front page, red headlines and a racy section called The Green Flash. The News, a Scripps-Howard rag, featured a lighthouse on the front page and the proud words, "Give Light and the People Will Find Their Own Way." The only light The News gave was when it was used to start a fire.

We hung out at Breen's and the Bay City Grill and talked newspapers 20 hours a day, sleeping four and needing even less. **Benny Horne** of the News was saluted for coining the term "Cow Palace." **Dick Nolan** and **Prescott Sullivan**, another guy with a hat on the back of his head and a cigar screwed into a corner of his mouth, was king of the sports

columnists. At The Chronicle, "boy wonder" editor, **Paul Smith**, came and went but left his mark — a fine young staff and a much improved paper. I was only a kid columnist, in awe of such great reporters as **Dick Hyer** and **Al Hyman**, **Harry Lerner** and **Carolyn Anspacher, Ed Montgomery** and a very young **Art Hoppe. Bill Wren** waved a fistful of green stuff and stole me away to The Examiner. "When you were with The Chronicle," he said by way of greeting, "I thought you wrote the worst goddam column I ever read. Now that you're with us, I think it's the greatest."

Enter **Scott Newhall** as The Chron's editor. He took a guy named **Charles McCabe** who knew nothing about sports and made him a sports columnist. In male chauvinism's last gasp, he turned a former hairdresser into **Count Marco**, who put down women. A dancer named **Terrence O'Flaherty** turned out to be a bitch of a TV columnist. **Art Hoppe** became the best satirist in the business, better than Buchwald or Russell Baker. I got my old corner back, and **Stanton Delaplane** continued stringing pearls of prose. Now Del and McCabe are gone, O'Flaherty and Count Marco are long retired, we're down to two papers and I'm going out for a toast to the memories that bless and burn.

Reporter and columnist Stanton Delaplane spoons dessert into the mouth of an apparently sated Herb during a media cruise, above. The two journalists before the junket, circa 1960, previous page.

San Francisco Chronicle Editor Paul C. Smith, who had hired the young Herb Caen, climbs a Death Valley monument (above) with the paper's Executive Editor Scott Newhall in February 1958. The Chronicle trumpets the return of its prodigal son from the competing San Francisco Examiner in January 1958, above right.

William Randolph Hearst wooed Herb away from the Chronicle to the competing Examiner in 1950. Legend has it that as many as 30,000 readers switched to the Examiner, and left a columnar void The Chronicle tried vainly to fill for the next eight years. Robert de Roos, a veteran reporter selected to write a competing column with young legman Pierre Salinger, remembers what it was like to go up against a giant: "The unthinkable happened. Herb Caen, the brilliant columnist, the biggest circulation draw in Northern California, a mainstay of the paper, left to go to The Examiner. This must have devastated Paul Smith, who had discovered and nurtured Herb. Perhaps the shock addled his brain: He tapped me to replace Caen. Sending me against Herb was like

throwing rocks at Gibraltar, sending a guppy out to battle a shark; I was like David without a sling. I tried to refuse. No luck. Finally, I said, 'All right, Paul, but I'm not Herb Caen and never will be.' The column was passable, but proved beyond a doubt that I was not Herb Caen and never would be."

When the column was in its infancy, Herb dreamed up a character named *Effie Zilch*, the average San Francisco reader to whom the column should appeal. Effie lived in the Sunset. After sending her husband off to work every morning, she would make herself a fresh pot of coffee, put her slippered feet up on the table, and read The Chronicle, always starting with Herb Caen. When Herb or Jerry Bundsen were iffy about an item, they would ask each other, "Would Effie Zilch go for this?" and if the item didn't pass the Zilch test, it got tossed. This went on for decades.

Our Native Witz

On September 17, 1972, Caen's column introduced one of his most enduring contributors, Strange de Jim: "I didn't believe in reincarnation in any of my other lives, and I don't see why I should have to believe in it in this one." Herb received hundreds of quotes (he printed more than 300) over the next 25 years, always on letterhead reading "From the desk of Strange de Jim," with no return address. For more than 15 years Herb didn't know the identity of Strange, who only called himself "San Francisco's Official Fool." Strange was a highly visible character, writing articles for other publications, and often appearing in public—but always with a pillowcase over his head (sometimes inprinted with "Strange de Jim slept here"). In 1987 Herb and Strange met briefly at Barnaby Conrad's Santa Barbara Writers' Conference, but they still kept up their "anonymous" relationship.

Strange de Jim at the Old Poodle Dog: "I won't eat snails—I prefer fast food."

JULY 15, 1985

* * *

80-something Cyril Magnin, San Francisco's Official Greeter, had attended Steve Silver's local musical comedy extravaganza several hundred times.
Strange de Jim's strange ambition: "I want to be there the night Cyril Magnin realizes he's already *seen* 'Beach Blanket Babylon.'"

JULY 27, 1985

* * *

"Monogamous," foolosophizes Strange de Jim, "is what one partner in every relationship wants it to be."

FEBRUARY 3, 1986

Gertrude Stein didn't like Oakland because there's no there there. Strange de Jim explains that he likes San Francisco because "there's so much here here."

FEBRUARY 18, 1986

* * *

"Last week I really got burnt, I went to a discount massage parlor, and it turned out to be self-service."

JUNE 2, 1981

* * *

"Next thing you know, Reagan will be selling arms to the Venus de Milo."

DECEMBER 2, 1996

* * *

"No wonder I was always so confused in church, I assumed the Lord of Hosts referred to Johnny Carson."

JANUARY 21, 1987

Sporting Green headline: "Giants Lose An Ugly One." Strange de Jim: "Who'd they trade now?"

MARCH 15, 1989

* * *

"Ah yes, Morton Downey, Jr., sad evidence that evolution works much faster in reverse."

MAY 1, 1989

* * *

Did you take your medicine, grandma?: "Just think," muses Strange de Jim. "We're the first society to kill off our old people with childproof caps."

JUNE 23, 1989

* * *

Lurching on: "I've never understood food stamps, I didn't know poor people had that much food to mail in the first place."

JULY 29, 1983

A Caen Lexicon

Baghdad-by-the-Bay—San Francisco ● ● ● The City That Knows Chow ● ● ● The Muniserable Railway ● ● ● S.F. slot machines—the cable cars ● ● ● The Dambarcadero Freeway ● ● ● The 450 Suffer Building—The 450 Sutter medical building ● ● ● Glums—the opposite of gays ● ● ● Washbag—the Washington Square Bar & Grill ● ● ● There's no business like Joe business—all the restaurants named Joe's ● ● ● The car-strangled spanner—the Bay Bridge ● ● ● The Golden Great Bridge ● ● ● Berserkeley ● ● ● Italian-Swish Colony —Finocchio's ● ● ● Beatnik—coined in early 1958 just after Sputnik went up ● ● ● Hashbury—the Haight-Ashbury ● ● ● Hippo—a fat hippie ● ● ● Pernicious Armenia—what William Saroyan was suffering from ● ● ● The White Cliffs of Doelger—the outer Sunset District, built by Henry Doelger ● ● ● Bawdway—the Broadway strip joints ● ● ● Benny Bufoono—Beniamino Bufano, the great and ofttimes eccentric San Francisco sculptor ● ● ● San Francisco's alarm clock—the Ferry Building clock ● ● ● A sorry/full situation—downtown garages ● ● ● Mysterious East Bay—Oakland environs ● ● ● The Dread Piedmontese—inhabitants of Piedmont

The Item Smasher

It was remarkable how Herb put together a daily column of over 1,000 words and kept it as topical and entertaining as he did. He read the daily papers at home over his unvarying breakfast of Shredded Wheat and half a banana, then arrived at the office no later than 10 a.m. After checking dozens of phone calls and more than 100 letters that came each day, he would pick the stories he wanted for the next day, typing the basic information on 3x5 scraps of paper, which he placed in a small metal box he kept on his desk and referred to as the 'item smasher.' Around 11 a.m. he would go through all the items and pick out the sequence that suited him. Then he'd close the door. For the next hour and a half to two hours he'd be pecking out the column on the Royal. Occasionally we'd discover that an item had run in another publication and he'd make a substitution, but that didn't happen often. He claimed it took nothing more than his 'monkey mind' to organize the information. He loved to say that 'three-dot columns aren't written. They accumulate, like hash.'

Herb had myriad complaints about his beloved city, but few of these gripes had as long a history as his hatred of pigeons. At right, he lures them into his trap at Union Square in July 1960. His battle to free the city of the 'feathered rats' included kudos whenever anyone came up with a way to halt their proliferation—fake owls, grain laced with birdie birth control chemicals, even corn soaked in bourbon (which brought down the wrath of bird lovers and teetotalers everywhere). He cheered whenever a peregrine falcon family would nest downtown, and relished the items about watching the falcons swoop down on their slower prey.

Pigeon Poopulation

I was standing in line at Polk and California to see a new art movie and was spattered by pigeons. That's culture of a certain ordure, isn't it? Some misguided dogoodnik who lives above was feeding the pigeons, which I believe is a federal offense, at least. Apparently pigeons don't retain anything. Eat, splat, justlikethat. The crowd being shat upon was getting pretty angry and shouting threats at the feeder — "We gonna come up there and get you, man!" — but I took charge, as I always do, and calmed them down with tales of St. Francis' love of birds and how his habit had to be drycleaned every week at Meader's. The answer to the pigeon problem is birth control pills, which they've been using down at Balboa Park in San Diego the past two years and have cut the pigeon population from about 5,000 to 1,000! All pigeons, being perpetually horny, should be on the pill anyway, or my name isn't Charles Squab.

JUNE 18, 1989

In Three Acts

One of the great lies in the columnar world is "Reprinted by popular demand." In most cases, this is a ploy perpetrated by rogues and scoundrels who have a hangover or nothing to write about, or both. At the moment, I am suffering from neither affliction, but the truth is I have had several requests — not demands — that I reprint that "funny column" I did once about the opera. Since I have written any number of side-splittingly funny columns about the opera, it took me a while to decide which one they meant, and I finally settled on my all-purpose synopsis for any opera in three acts, four languages and five hours. I wrote it because so many opera lovers read the program after the event and are surprised to discover what they slept through. The opera is titled "Dristan and Clairol," with music by Guglielmo Flavorzone and a libretto by Samuel Sanskrit, based on a book by Enrico Banducci derived from a word uttered in 1836 by Sir Edmund Bore. Unfortunately, the word is unprintable.

....

Act I

As the curtain rises, Dristan makes a triumphal entrance, singing his famous hymn to Sol, king of the Bagels. Sol, the first basso (a role made famous by Guillermo McCovey), offers him the hand of his beautiful daughter, Clairol, in response to which Dristan sings, "Che bella, mais wo ist la miserare?" ("It's a nice hand, but how about a look at the rest of her?") Irium, knowing that Clairol is actually Baron Richard de Blum in drag, shouts the betrayal from the ranks of the peasants, and declares her love. Unfortunately, she herself is disguised as a donkey, being under a spell, and coughs constantly, having played a cigaret girl in "Carmen" once too often. She drops her handkerchief, which is picked up by Count Giuseppe DiMaggio, who has been discarded by Clairol, who has been rejected by Lentil, who has been imprisoned in a high dungeon by Sol, a secret member of the Giovanni Birchio Society. As the curtain falls, the skies darken, the plot sickens and the peasants are revolting, except for Clairol, who has fallen asleep in the arms of Nembutal.

....

Act II

In the mountain hideaway of Dreft, the fairy king, who performs a gay dance to the music of the Smugglers, a banjo band. Clairol, seeking her mother, Machree, has been rejected by Dristan, who has found her handkerchief in the possession of DiMaggio and has killed him in the same high dungeon where Machree is held prisoner. Clairol, still cough-ing, unaware that she has conspicuous consumption, sings "Come un bel di DiMaggio" and stumbles off, vowing to spend the rest of her life in Solitude or Penance, two retire-ment centers near Coalinga.

Dristan arrives with his faithful friend, Zinfandel, on a fish-ing expedition. Drawing a pike, he runs Dreft through, not realizing that Dreft is Irium in disguise. As Irium dies, she reveals that she is actually a prince and the son of Sol, king of the Bagels.

....

Act III

This act opens on a more relaxed note (B flat), as the morning newspaper critics have already left to make their deadlines. Dristan, miraculously saved from drowning by mouth-to-mouth resuscitation performed by the faithful Zin-fandel, is on his way to join a convent, having been turned into a woman by the evil witch, Kreplach, who is actually Machree, who has escaped from the dungeon disguised as an Elk (although in the original libretto she is a Rotarian). Dristan and Clairol declare their love for each other, after which Clairol reveals that she is actually Fluoristan, opening her mouth to show 33 percent fewer cavities.

As the revolting peasants begin to dance again, she is seized by another, and final, coughing spell, little knowing that help from Broemmel's Pharmacy is on the way. They vow to die together, and prepare a poisonous potion of gin and vermouth, which Dristan swallows first, singing in agony, "Troppo Cinzano!" ("Too much vermouth!"), in which she joins for the immortal duet, "Chiedi all' aura Noilly Prat'" ("So next time ask for something drier"). The potion having failed, they

climb to the top of the nearest basso profundo and, clasping hands, leap into the orchestra pit, there to perish among the oboes, one of which is actually Sol, king of the Bagels.

Onstage, as the curtain falls, the peasants are still revolting, and the audience sounds a little menacing, too.

OK, so it's not much of a story. Besides, the day or night of the synopsis may soon be over. With the advent of "supertitles," which appear above the proscenium arch — right, sleepyhead, up THERE — the bare bones of the plot are exposed in all their awful simplicity. "Hello." "Good-by." "Give my regards to France." It was better in the old days, believe me, when we all thought those dear souls onstage were singing their hearts out about something important. Have a nice season.

A stage hand moves crate past a huge mural for the opera "Rigoletto," 1990.

....
123

Saucy Sign

Outside Sukker's Likkers on Polkstrasse: "Sex Is Nobody's Business Except the Three People Involved."

FEBRUARY 13, 1980

Tales of the Town

Jeff Lyons, who works in the financial district, found himself stuck in a stalled elevator at 333 Bush with three fellow passengers, all women. He pressed the emergency button and on came a male voice asking "What's the problem?" Jeff: "I'm stuck in here with three women." Male voice, heartily: "Well, make the most of it till we get it fixed." Jeff, who's gay: "I don't go that way." Voice, after a moment's silence: "Uh — well, maybe you can pick up some fashion tips." Knock off the cracks about homophobes, buddy. Jeff thinks the story's hilarious.

JULY 18, 1988

Downhill Racer

"What do Tammy Bakker and Squaw Valley have in common? Six inches of base, six inches of powder, and lots of lift lines." Sadie, Sadie, the Rabbi Lady said that.

DECEMBER 27, 1987

Two members of Unity and More in '84 strut their stuff at that summer's Gay Freedom Day Parade.

Fun for Funds

"Nothing ever gets done in San Francisco," Reggie Jackson sneered recently. "The only thing the people like to do is go out to dinner and the Hookers Ball." Not too far off the mark, really. That's a fair metaphor for the endless round of fund-raising parties. Everybody's ready to play for pay — always in good cause, of course, but I never met a hooker who didn't think her cause was just, too.

DECEMBER 20, 1980

A mock protester at the 1986 Gay Freedom Day Parade, below.

Man the Barricades

Fred Goerner's scooplet: He hears that the Pacific-Union Club has finally knuckled under to feminist pressure and put in a women's exercise room. Equipment installed so far: two ironing boards and a vacuum cleaner . . .

JULY 15, 1988

. . .

125

"I will miss Herb.
He had the twinkliest
eyes, the readiest smile
and the twiggiest legs
on the tennis court."
— MAGGIE EASTWOOD

"He was a complex guy. He was approaching 70 when he first appeared at practice in full Giants' uniform and properly oiled first baseman's mitt. He was our starting first baseman when we beat a strong New York team featuring former minor leaguer Mario Cuomo.

During one of our media softball games of the Democratic Convention, we played against Tom Brokaw's team. They were a lot younger than us. Herb played first base, and he was really run down by this roughneck from The New York Times. Really thrown on the asphalt. It looked like he was really hurt so I said, 'C'mon Herb, I'm taking you out of the game.' And he got really hot. He gave me the look that chilled men's souls, and he said, 'No way! I'm staying in, Moose!' Case closed.

A week later I asked him how he was feeling and he said, 'Fine! Fine!' Now, I'm getting older myself, and I know if you hit the concrete like that, you're going to hurt for a week or so. But he wouldn't admit it. That must be part of the reason he could write that column six days a week. He was incredibly tough. He had to be."

— ED MOOSE

Herb beats Fearless Spectator
columnist Charles McCabe in the
outfield during a 1962 game, above.

Throwing the first pitch for the
Giants home opener against
Houston at Candlestick Park
in 1986, left.

Herb's Favorite Toast

Here's to the roses and lilies in bloom,
You in my arms and I in your room,
A door that is locked, a key that is lost,
A bird and a bottle and a bed badly tossed,
And a night that is 50 years long.

in Ranch Mi...

s Venetian Room... Yet ano...

ony" (real name John Joseph Vidal Sr.) "...

World Boxing Hall of Fame and a familiar figure i...

was a major sport here. He wore a carnation daily

pretty girl he saw he saw.

(STREET SCENES: stardash...

heavy traffic: the driver of a Smart Food Popcorn

dle lane, making a deal with the driver in the ti...

ting an armload of popcorn, the latter allowed

his right turn... They do things different

took a ride on the freeway with h...

82-

and as she was about to change lane

down there, and as she was about to change lane

"It's what you say down here -- 'S'

for look over your shoulder,

Sonora Unio

football games with the hila...

smile? If I get a vote for Stockton's su...

Papa. Voice, smarts, wit long-overdue co...

today's opening of his ... And Sports & Boat Show a...

consecutive year. Ol' Kangarooney, as we call him...

Sonoma till they beat him up once too often) has...

around here... (for a dog-bites-man award,...

headline "Hallinan Sworn In as D.A. -- Vows To Be...

Bernstein likes the double bill on the marquee of...

"The American President -- Waiting to Exhale."

HERBASIDES: Leslie Caron fans may want to know...

a's in Palo Alto tonight at 6 for dinner before...

"Gigi" at the Stanford Theater at 8... stardash...

staurant in Paris... M...

y-restored